THE HIDDEN
WORLD
OF FORCES

THE HIDDEN WORLD OF FORCES

Jack R. White

Illustrated with photographs and diagrams

G.P. PUTNAM'S SONS   New York

Library of Congress Cataloging-in-Publication Data
White, Jack R.   The Hidden World of Forces/
Jack R. White.   p. cm.   Reprint. Originally
published: New York: Dodd, Mead, © 1987.
Includes index.   Summary: Discusses some
of the forces at work in the universe, such as
electromagnetism, gravitation, surface tension,
and friction, with illustrative experiments.
1. Force and energy—Juvenile literature.
[1. Force and energy.]   I. Title.
[QC73.4.W47   1989] 531—dc19 89-3658 CIP AC
ISBN 0-399-61247-5
10 9 8 7 6 5 4 3

DEDICATED TO ALL THE YOUNG PEOPLE WHOSE IMAGINATION
AND CURIOSITY LETS THEM SEE THE MANY WONDERS HIDDEN
IN PLAIN SIGHT AROUND THEM

CONTENTS

1

Life in a Force Field

All around us, unseen and often unnoticed, is a world of controlled violence. At every instant, powerful forces are at work pulling or pushing on every object in the universe. From the smallest of particles within the nuclei of atoms, to the most enormous of galaxies, to ourselves, all matter is controlled, shaped, and held together by invisible forces.

If even one of these forces were somehow taken away, the universe as we know it would come apart. Take away the force of gravitation and our solar system would self-destruct. Everything on the surface of the earth, including the oceans and the air, would be launched into space. Earth would break free of the sun. The sun and the stars would cease to shine and their matter would pour out into space. The earth itself would fly apart and become a cloud of dust.

Take away the force of electromagnetism and matter itself would come apart. Within the atoms that make up all matter, electromagnetism binds electrons to the nuclei. It also ties

At every instant, powerful forces are at work pushing or pulling on every object in the universe. The force of *gravitation* reaches across the vastness of space to hold this comet in its orbit around the sun.

atoms together into molecules and ties molecules together into larger structures of matter.

Matter gets its characteristics from these ties. Stone is hard and cotton is soft. Air is a gas and water is (usually) a liquid. Your shirt is red or white or yellow, and pickles taste the way they do because of the kinds of molecules of matter and the way that they are bound together. Take away the force of electromagnetism and there would be no matter as we now know it.

THE NATURE OF FORCE

What is a force? A basic definition is any push or pull. Force is often tied to motion. Some force is needed to start a baseball moving, for example. But force can be present even when there is no motion. A book lying on a table is being pulled downward by the force of gravity, but it is not moving.

Every force has two properties: strength and direction. The book is being pulled downward by gravity with a strength equal to its weight. To pick the book up, you must apply a force in the opposite direction that has a strength greater than the weight of the book. Forces also have one other property. With one important exception, they are invisible. We can often see what a force does, but not the force itself. The exception is light. Did you know that light is one kind of force?

Gravitation and electromagnetism are two of the four known *fundamental* forces. They are the only fundamental forces that we experience directly. The other two are called the "strong" nuclear force and the "weak" nuclear force.

10

The "strong" force holds the nuclei of atoms together. The "weak" force is involved in radioactive decay. Both have extremely short distances and much less is known about them than about gravitation and electromagnetism.

From the fundamental forces of gravitation and electromagnetism come dozens of secondary forces. These secondary forces are probably as familiar to us as gravity. You see their effects at work in dozens of ways every day, perhaps without realizing that a force is at work. Did you know, for example, that raindrops are formed by a force?

A LIFETIME OF EXPERIMENTS

Forces are not just something to read about. You can do experiments with many forces yourself. For each force discussed in this book, there are experiments that you can do, using common materials such as water, rubber bands, paper clips, and balloons.

Experiments are the best way to see cause and effect. They demonstrate better than any amount of words how a certain force causes an effect to happen. From these experiments, you may discover some new ways of thinking about forces and some new connections between forces and everyday experience. You will probably find that you knew a lot more about forces than you may have thought.

Perhaps without realizing it, you have been experimenting with forces all your life. Learning to pick up objects, to drink through a straw, to walk, to ride a bicycle, to skate, to throw a ball or a Frisbee, and to fly a kite or a paper airplane are just a few examples.

We use forces to connect and interact with the world

around us. We never stop learning about forces, although we are not usually conscious of this learning and we rarely try to describe these "experiments" in words. Let's take a look now at some of the familiar forces that we will be investigating in the chapters of this book.

A WORLD OF FORCES

Gravitation is perhaps the most familiar of all forces. We struggle against its pull all our lives. Only divers, with their weight supported by the water, and astronauts in orbit have experienced long periods without feeling the pull of gravity. As familiar as it is, gravitation is one of the least understood of all forces. In ways that are difficult for us to imagine, gravitation curves space and causes time to slow down.

The force of *buoyancy* that makes boats float and helium

The force of *buoyancy* causes ships to float and balloons, such as this hot-air balloon, to rise.

The force of *lift* is able to make "thin air" support the enormous weight of a large jetliner.

and hot-air balloons rise is caused by gravity. It may seem a little strange that the force of gravity pulling downward causes things to rise, but that is exactly what happens.

There are also forces created by motion. Have you ever wondered what makes an airplane fly? Airplanes fly because of a force known as *lift*. Lift is created around objects when they move through a gas or a liquid or when a gas or a liquid flows around them. The secret of flight is learning to control the force of lift.

Can you hear force? Yes, in a way. When something moves or disturbs the air, force is transferred from the object to the air and is carried by the air in waves. When the force of these waves strikes your eardrums, they cause your eardrums to move with the same patterns of motion as the object that disturbed the air. We call these patterns sound.

Electromagnetism in its forms of electricity and magnetism is responsible for much of the technology of the twentieth century. It is the source of our long-distance communication by radio, television, and telephone. It is also the source of power for heating, lighting, and electric motors.

Can you see force? In a way. The light that your eyes see is electromagnetic radiation that travels in waves of magnetic and electric force. Did you know that sunlight pushes on you with a tiny force?

Surface tension is a strange force that pulls liquids into little balls. It is a secondary force caused by electromagnetism. Surface tension is the force that causes rain to fall in drops instead of as clouds of steam. Surface tension has the strength to support small pieces of metal, yet you can make it virtually disappear in an instant with just a drop of detergent, as you will see in an experiment.

The electromagnetic force binding molecules at the surfaces of two different objects prevents one from sliding smoothly over the other and creates the force we call *friction*. Friction opposes motion and causes almost everything that moves to wear.

Friction is usually the enemy of machines, but it would be difficult for us to survive without it. Without friction, every surface would be more slippery than the smoothest ice, and walking or even standing would be almost impossible. Imagine trying to eat food so slippery it wouldn't stay on your fork.

THE KEYS TO THE UNIVERSE

A large part of science and engineering is devoted to the study of forces. The science of chemistry is based on the forces between atoms and molecules of matter and the bonds

14

The force of *surface tension* causes water to pull together into tiny round drops.

that they form. The science of physics is largely devoted to forces and the energy that creates them. Physicists try to learn the causes of forces and understand how they interact with matter. Research into the mysteries of the fundamental

15

forces takes physicists into the very deepest mysteries of the universe .

Physics is the basis for all the branches of engineering, especially mechanical, aeronautical, and electrical engineering. Engineers create the designs for new machines and devices that use force in their operation.

Understanding how force is used is often the key to understanding how a machine works. But forces are not just used in man-made devices. Understanding forces is often the key to unlocking nature's secrets as well. Plants and animals use forces in ingenious ways to survive.

In the chapters ahead, we will investigate some of the more familiar forces that you are likely to encounter and use everyday. We will see what causes them and how they act. We will find examples of their use around the house, and we will do some experiments to see how they really work. Let's begin our exploration of the hidden world of forces.

2

Force, Molecules, Matter, and Mass

Earth, air, fire, and water. The ancient Greeks believed these were the four forms of matter. The Greeks were at least partly right in their thinking. Today, we know that matter is found in three different forms: as a solid, as a liquid, or as a gas. (Earth, water, and air qualify as solid, liquid, and gas, but the flame of a fire is mostly gas.)

Every person has a lot of experience with matter in all three forms. The book you are holding is a solid, the air you are breathing is a gas, and the water you drink is a liquid. Water, by the way, is the only common substance that is familiar in all three forms; as ice, water, and steam.

The smallest bits of matter are *atoms*. Atoms are tied to other atoms by the electromagnetic force to make larger particles called *molecules*. The solid, liquid, or gas form of any kind of matter is determined by the way in which its molecules are linked together.

FORCE IN SOLIDS

If the molecules are so firmly tied together that they are not free to move about, the material will be a solid. Because

17

each of its molecules is held fixed in place by bonds of force to surrounding molecules, a solid keeps its shape. The shape of a solid can only be changed if an outside force presses on the material strongly enough to break apart the bonds between the molecules.

The form of matter determines how it transmits force. A solid nail carries force directly through from the head to the point. A liquid or a gas, such as the air in a balloon, spreads force over the area of its container as pressure.

Because it keeps its shape, a solid object transmits force through it directly. If you press on one side of a block of wood with a force of five pounds, for example, then a force of five pounds will be carried through the block to the opposite side. Strike the head of a nail with a hammer and the force of the blow will be carried through the nail to its point and the point will be driven into the wood.

FORCE IN LIQUIDS

If the molecules of a material are bound together, but not held tightly in place, the material will be a liquid. Liquids take on the shape of their container. In fact, they must have a container to hold them. Liquids are only slightly compressible. When put under pressure, they change their volume very little because the bonds between the molecules prevent them from being more tightly packed.

Because the molecules of a liquid are free to move about, an outside force is not transmitted directly through a liquid as it is with a solid. Imagine pressing down with your hand on water in a bowl. Very little force would be carried through the liquid. The molecules of water would simply move aside and around your hand, leaving you with a wet hand.

FORCE IN GASES

In a gas, the molecules are much more loosely connected than in a liquid. They are not only free to move around each other, they are also free to move apart from each other. In fact, the molecules of a gas are continually in motion, colliding with other molecules and with the walls of their container.

Because of this freedom, gases take on the full shape of their container and must be enclosed on all sides. The freedom of the molecules to move farther apart or closer together makes gases compressible. Under pressure, a gas shrinks in volume. When released, it expands. Like liquids, gases don't transmit force directly as solids do. Imagine pushing on air, for example.

These different solid, liquid, or gas forms of matter determine the way force is carried through a material and whether it is concentrated in a small area or distributed over a large area. Let's look at this force transmission in solids first.

FORCE, AREA, AND PRESSURE

You know to be careful with sharp objects. It only takes a small force pushing on a needle or the point of a tack to stick your finger. But you can press the open palm of your hand against a wall or other flat surface with all your strength and not be hurt.

What is the difference? Why is a needle "sharp" and a wall not? Since a wall is very much larger than the point of a needle, it is an easy guess that sharpness must have something to do with size.

A thumbtack makes a good example. A thumbtack has a large "head" on one end and a small point on the other. The tack is a solid, so when you press on a thumbtack, the tack carries the force through it. The force of your thumb pressing on the head is the same as the force of the point

20

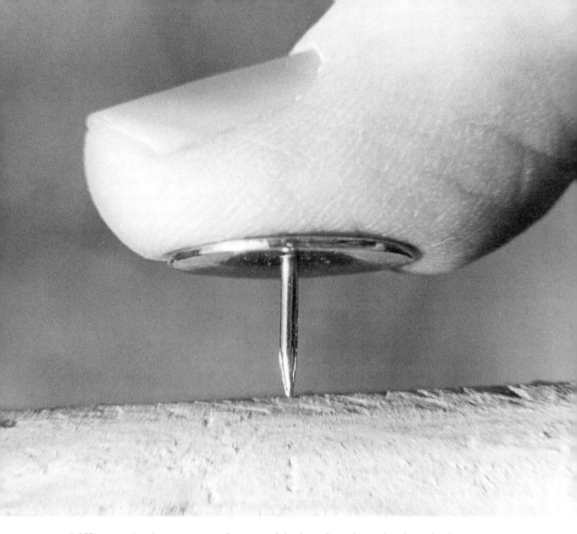

Different sized areas are often used in hand tools and other devices to multiply force of pressure. A thumbtack is made with a large area at its head and a very small area at its point to multiply pressure.

against the board. The difference (and the reason why the point sticks into the board and the head does not stick into your thumb) has to do with area and pressure.

The *area* of a surface is simply its size in two dimensions. For a surface that is shaped like a rectangle, the area is the length multiplied by the width. Area has an enormous effect on the way force is applied. A small area concentrates force. A large area distributes it; spreads it out.

The tiny point of a thumbtack concentrates force so that it is able to break apart the bonds that hold the molecules of wood together (or the molecules of your finger if you press against the point!). That is what is happening when the point sticks into something.

Force spread over an area is called *pressure*. Pressure, force, and area are related in the following way: pressure is the strength of the force divided by the size of the surface area (Pressure = Force ÷ Area). It is the amount of force in each unit of area.

USING AREA TO MULTIPLY PRESSURE

If the amount of force is kept the same, but the area is made very small, then the pressure becomes very large. Likewise, if the area is made large, the pressure becomes small. A thumbtack, being large on one end and small on the other, acts as a kind of pressure transformer or pressure multiplier. It changes a low pressure on the thumb end into a high pressure on the pointed end.

This kind of pressure multiplication is used in all sorts of hand tools. Look around your home and you will probably be able to find several tools that use this principle. A knife, for example, usually has a handle with a fairly large surface area and a blade with an edge that has a very small area. When we sharpen a knife, we are making the area of the cutting edge even smaller so that, for the same force, the pressure at the edge will be much greater.

22

USING AREA TO MULTIPLY FORCE

Because liquids and gases can change their shape, they don't transmit force directly and we can't use area to multiply pressure. Suppose we put a liquid or a gas into a closed container so that we can apply force by "squeezing." The movement of the molecules spreads the applied force evenly over the sides, top, and bottom of the container, so that all parts of the container have the same pressure.

With solids, we saw that pressure is equal to the force *divided* by the surface area. In liquids and gases, we usually turn this formula around and find the force that is made by a certain pressure. This gives force as the pressure *multiplied* by the area (Force = Pressure × Area).

We saw how different areas on solid hand tools are used to multiply pressure. With liquids and gases, which keep the same pressure throughout, different sized areas can be used to multiply force.

You can probably think of several examples where the area of a solid is made larger or smaller to be able to get more or less force from a liquid or gas. A sailboat, for example, uses sails to change the pressure caused by the wind into a force to push the sailboat through the water. In a high wind, when the pressure is greater, a sailboat uses smaller sails. In a light breeze, sailors hoist larger sails to get a greater force.

One example is a tire pump and a bicycle tire. You could pump up a bicycle tire with a hand pump while a 75-kilogram (165-pound) man sat on the bicycle (although you might suggest that he get off and help you pump). You wouldn't want to try to lift this much weight directly yourself, but with air pressure, you can do it.

The force you apply pressing down on the handle of the pump is spread over the small area of a piston inside the pump. A hose connects the pump with the tire, so the pressure is the same inside the tire as inside the pump.

But the tire has a much larger area. Since force equals pressure times area, the tire can lift a much greater force than you are having to push down on the pump handle. This smaller area to larger area connection acts as a force multiplier.

FORCE AND MOTION: MECHANICS

One of the earliest things that we discover about force as a child is that force makes things happen. Push or pull on something hard enough and it will usually move. Apply force, using the muscles of your arm, and you can send a ball sailing through the air. Apply a greater force and you can throw it at a greater speed.

In science, it is not enough just to know that something happens. We need to know the amounts. Exactly how much force causes how much motion? We must know mathematically how force and motion are related. Only then can we start to understand why things behave as they do and, from that, be able to apply this understanding to other, greater problems.

The relationship between force and motion is the subject of a branch of the science of physics known as *mechanics* and it is one of the oldest of the sciences. We started this chapter with ancient Greek ideas about matter. The first writings about force and motion also come from ancient Greece, from the philosopher, Aristotle, who lived from 384 to 322 B.C.

Aristotle's theories on force and motion were taught in most of the schools and universities of Europe for almost 2,000 years, up into the early 1600s. This seems a remarkably long time to us today, when we see new ideas in science replacing old ones almost continually.

It seems even more remarkable when you realize that many of Aristotle's ideas were wrong. He believed, incorrectly, that force and speed were directly related and he thought that a steady force was necessary to keep an object moving at the same speed.

GALILEO AND NEWTON

These ideas were corrected by perhaps the two greatest scientists in history: Galileo Galilei in Italy and, following his death, Sir Isaac Newton in England. In the late 1500s, Galileo proved that force does not directly control the speed of an object. Rather, force causes an *acceleration*. Acceleration is any change in the speed or in the direction that an object is moving.

Newton expanded Galileo's findings and put them into mathematical form as physical laws of motion. Newton's first law of motion says that an object will stay at rest, not moving, unless some outside force pushes or pulls on it. If the object is already moving, no force is needed to keep it moving. It will continue to move at the same speed and in the same direction unless some force acts on it.

However, in most real situations, some force is needed to

keep an object moving because there is always some drag or friction that acts to slow an object down. An outside force is needed to overcome the friction. Galileo and Newton were able to imagine a perfect environment without any friction. They separated the action of friction from that of other forces.

MASS AND WEIGHT

Newton's first law describes an object without any forces pushing or pulling on it. For this law, it doesn't matter how massive the object is. Newton's second law describes what happens to an object when some force is applied. Before Newton could make this connection between force and motion, he needed a way to describe the amount of material in an object.

You know that it takes more force to throw an iron ball than a tennis ball. An iron ball is heavier than a tennis ball, but it is not the weight that makes it harder to throw. If there were no gravity, so that the balls had no weight, the iron ball would still be harder to throw. The iron ball has a greater amount of matter or material in it and matter resists being accelerated. Newton called the measure of the amount of material in an object its *mass.*

Mass (the resistance to being accelerated) and *weight* (the force of the earth's gravity pulling on an object) are often confused, even by scientists and engineers, but they are quite different things. An object has the same mass everywhere in the universe. It has weight only where there is gravity.

Mass and weight are often mixed up because, on earth,

26

The mass of an object such as a brick resists acceleration (any change
in the speed or the direction of motion). The greater the mass, the
greater the force that is needed to accelerate it.

27

they are directly related. Objects with a greater mass have a greater weight in direct proportion. An object with twice the mass weighs twice as much. Because mass and weight are so directly connected, we often interchange one for the other without being aware of the difference.

Even the different units used for weight and mass can be confusing. In the English system of units, weight is measured in *pounds* and mass in *slugs*. On the surface of the earth, one slug weighs 32.17 pounds. In the metric system, weight is measured in *newtons* and mass in *kilograms*. On earth, one kilogram weighs 9.807 newtons.

If you step onto a scales in the United States, where the English system is still widely used, the scales will measure the force of gravity on your body (your weight) in pounds. Mass is rarely used.

However, if you stepped onto a scales in Europe or Japan, where the metric system is used, the scales would probably give your mass in kilograms. Although it is the force of your weight that causes the scales to register a reading, the dial is marked in kilograms.

NEWTON'S SECOND LAW

Newton's second law of motion says that force is equal to mass times acceleration (Force = Mass × Acceleration). This tells how much force there is when a certain amount of mass is accelerated. We can also turn this formula around to find the amount of acceleration that a force will give to a certain mass (Acceleration = Force ÷ Mass).

A mathematical formula such as this is valuable because it tells the exact relationship between the different quantities.

If you double the amount of mass, for example, then it will take twice the force to give it the same acceleration. Also, if any two of the quantities in the formula are known, the other can be calculated.

For example, if the force and the acceleration are known, the mass can be calculated. This is how the mass of objects like the earth, moon, and sun have been found. Imagine trying to "weigh" the earth (actually to find its mass) any other way.

We will take a much closer look at weight and what it means in the next chapter when we investigate what is perhaps the most interesting and puzzling force of all: the force of gravitation.

3

The Grandest Force of All: Gravitation

"How much do you weigh?"

That seems like a simple question. Most of us step onto a scales from time to time and we have some idea of our weight. Measuring weight is fairly simple, but what about the force that causes it? You may be surprised to learn that this familiar force that you can measure with a bathroom scales is one of the least understood of all. This is the force of gravitation, commonly called the force of gravity.

Gravitation is one of the four known fundamental forces. Unlike the other three (electromagnetism and the "strong" and "weak" nuclear forces), gravitation is extremely weak for tiny particles of atomic and molecular size. So much so, that scientists doing atomic research usually don't consider gravitation in their studies.

Gravitation's most spectacular work is done on the cosmic scale, where stars are created and destroyed by its force. For objects the size of planets and suns, its force is enormously strong. The strength of its force drops rapidly with increasing distance, but never completely vanishes. There may be no place in the universe that is totally without gravity.

On earth, gravity shapes our lives and our environment in countless ways. Every movement we make is a struggle against its force. Everything around us—the buildings, people, automobiles, oceans, and even the air we breathe—is held to the earth by gravity. Your home and everything in it, from tables and chairs to bowls and cups and spoons are all designed for living in earth's gravitational field.

Because gravity is so much a part of our lives, we don't often stop to wonder why we have weight. We seem to be pulled down toward the center of the earth as if we were bits of iron attracted to some kind of giant magnet. No one knows exactly why.

Secondary forces can be explained by the action of fundamental forces. Gravitation, being a fundamental force, doesn't depend on any other force for its actions. Searching for the "why" of a fundamental force comes close to searching for the very "why" of the universe itself.

GRAVITY AND MASS

Probably the most basic thing that we notice about the force of gravity on ourselves and the things around us is that the force is different for different objects. Some things weigh more than others. An adult weighs more than a baby, for example, and an automobile more than a bicycle. Gravity is selective: it pulls strongly on some things, weakly on others.

Weight is often connected with size, but it is not only size. It is the total amount and kind of material or matter that decides an object's weight. As we saw earlier, the term that is used to describe an amount of matter that includes its size, kind, and how it is packed is *mass*. The greater the mass, the greater the force of gravity on that object.

Once again, we find a connection between force and mass. We found that matter resists being accelerated and the greater the mass, the greater the force that will be needed to accelerate it. Now we discover that matter has yet another

Force and mass are connected in two ways: by gravity and by acceleration. You can feel these two forces at work on an object such as a book by feeling its weight pulling downward, and by feeling the force needed to swing the book back and forth.

property: its attraction by gravity. The more matter there is, the greater is the force of gravity on that object.

You can easily experience these two properties of matter for yourself. Pick up something fairly heavy, such as a book, and hold it out at arm's length. Feel the force of gravity pulling it downward? The strength of that force depends upon the book's mass and the strength of earth's gravity.

Now, rapidly swing the book back and forth, from side to side. Feel the force that your arm and wrist must apply to the book to stop its motion in one direction and speed it back the other way? The strength of that force depends upon the book's mass and the amount you accelerate it. Mass is the common link between the force of attraction of gravity and the force needed for acceleration.

From the earliest times, most scientists who studied the relationship between force and motion in the science of mechanics also studied the effects of gravity. The names of Aristotle, Galileo, and Newton appear again in this chapter and to this list we will add that of another great scientist, Albert Einstein.

ARISTOTLE, GALILEO, AND CONSTANT ACCELERATION

Aristotle believed that objects fell toward earth because the center of the earth was their "natural" resting place, and he believed that heavier objects fell faster than lighter ones. Like his ideas on mechanics, Aristotle's ideas on gravity were challenged by Galileo.

In a famous experiment, Galileo is said to have dropped two large stones (some stories say two iron cannon balls), one weighing ten times the other, from the top of the Leaning Tower of Pisa. It is not certain that he really did such a public experiment, but he probably did perform many similar experiments in private.

If the story is true, it is likely that most of the people watching expected the heavier stone to fall faster. Our "common sense" makes us feel that heavy objects should fall faster than light ones. The force of gravity pulling the heavier stone is greater and it seems natural that this greater force should make it fall faster.

But that is not how gravity works, and the people must have been surprised to see both stones strike the ground at the same time. Except for differences caused by air resistance, all objects gain speed at the same rate no matter what their weight. The acceleration is the same for all objects because of the dual property of mass.

A greater mass does give an object a greater weight pulling it downward, but a greater mass also has a greater *resistance to acceleration*. The two opposing effects balance, to give a constant acceleration. If you drop a heavy object and a light one from a high place, they will strike the ground at the same time. That is, they will unless the air slows one more than the other. A feather doesn't fall as fast as a stone in air, but it would fall just as fast in a vacuum.

SLOWING ACCELERATION DOWN

Galileo probably did very few experiments with free-falling objects because the high speeds make it difficult to tell what is happening. There were no clocks in Galileo's time that could accurately measure the fractions of a second

34

Gravity accelerates all masses the same—or would, if there were no air resistance. Caught in midair by the camera's shutter, a light tennis ball and a heavy wooden croquet ball fall to earth together.

needed for those speeds. So Galileo slowed acceleration down by doing most of his experiments on an *inclined plane*. An inclined plane is just a board or floor or other surface that is tilted so that it is slanting.

Galileo rolled balls down a slanting board and marked and measured the distance traveled in equal amounts or intervals of time. He found that the distance a ball traveled increased by an ever greater amount in each time interval. He calculated the speed and found that the speed increased by the same amount in each time interval. A constant gain in speed means a constant acceleration. Galileo found that the acceleration caused by gravity is always constant, no matter how heavy the object.

PENDULUMS

Pendulums are one of the most common examples of gravity accelerating heavy and light objects at the same rate. The back and forth swing of the pendulums that you see in "grandfather" clocks help the clock keep accurate time. Pendulums are usually made quite heavy, but the rate of the swing has nothing to do with weight.

The time it takes for a pendulum to make one back and forth swing (called the *period*) is set by the pendulum's length. A long pendulum will take longer to make a complete swing than a short pendulum. If you have a chance to go into a store that sells pendulum clocks, notice the speeds of the pendulums in different clocks.

Try an experiment with pendulums yourself with weights and pieces of string. Compare the time of swing of two pendulums of the same length, but with different weights tied on the string. Then see what happens with the same weights, but different lengths of string. You will find that the longer the string, the longer the period of the pendulum.

OF APPLES AND THE MOON

In the summer of 1666, a young man in England happened to see an apple fall from a tree in his mother's orchard and that simple event started a chain of ideas and discoveries that revolutionized the science of astronomy. The young man's name was Isaac Newton.

Newton later wrote, "And the same year, I began to think of gravity extending to the orb of the Moon . . ." Newton guessed that the same force that pulled the apple down from the tree also reached to the moon and held it in its orbit, and he set out to prove this mathematically.

The story of the falling apple is one that Newton told friends many years later. A falling apple may have helped spark the idea, but he had been thinking of the orbits of the moon and planets for some time before that. And when Newton thought about a problem in science or mathematics, he did so with a determination that kept him at work night and day, often forgetting to eat or sleep, until he had a solution.

Of course, Newton didn't discover gravity. From the work of Galileo and many others, the effects of gravity on objects on earth were well known. Also well known were the motions of the planets. What Newton discovered was a mathematical formula that describes the strength of the force pulling two objects together. His formula is now known as the Law of Universal Gravitation.

THE LAW OF GRAVITY

Newton concluded that the force of gravity between any two objects depends on two things: (1) on the amount of mass in the two objects and (2) on the distance between them. The force becomes stronger with greater mass and weaker with greater distance.

The strength of the force depends on the product of the two masses, that is, on the mass of one object multiplied by the mass of the other. If you double the mass of either object, you double the strength of the force.

The strength of the force pulling two objects together becomes weaker by the square of the distance, that is, by the distance multiplied by itself. If you double the distance between two objects, for example, the force of attraction between them drops to one-fourth of its first value.

Newton's formula also contains another term needed to make the different units of mass and distance come out correctly in units of force. This term is called the *gravitational*

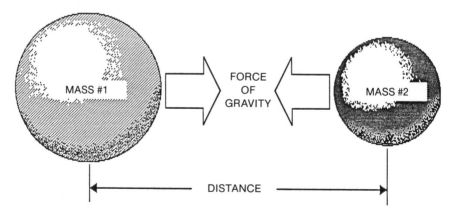

Every mass is attracted to every other mass. The force of gravity between any two objects depends on the amount of mass in them and the distance between them.

constant. Newton found the general relationship, but the actual value of the gravitational constant was not measured accurately until 1798, seventy-one years after his death.

As a mathematical statement, the Law of Universal Gravitation says several important things. It says that gravity is a mutual attraction, that is, it works both ways. While the earth's mass pulls you toward its center, your mass is pulling on the earth by the same amount that the earth is pulling on you. If you jump up and down, you can't make the earth move by any measurable amount because its mass is so much greater than yours, but the force is really there.

It also says that the attraction is not just to the earth. Every mass is attracted to every other mass. If you walk by a building, the building exerts a slight pull on your body and you exert a pull on the building. The building's pull is far too weak for you to feel, but it is large enough to be measured with sensitive instruments.

The great power of a mathematical formula such as Newton's is its ability to be applied to cases and problems that have not actually been experienced. Newton's formula tells the exact strength of the force for every possible combination of mass and distance, not just for those few examples that have been tested.

It is difficult for us today to appreciate the impact Newton's discovery had on astronomy. Almost overnight, astronomy was changed into a different kind of science. It had been a science without a theory that explained why the moon and planets travel in the paths they do. Astronomers and mathematicians searched for patterns in the information gathered from many observations. They knew how the heavenly bodies moved, but not why.

From Newton's time onward, astronomy has been a science based on mathematical models and theories that astronomers compare with their actual observations. Newton made the mysterious motions of the stars and planets seem as ordered and as open to understanding as the motions of the wheels within a mechanical clock.

THE LIMITS OF NEWTON'S LAW

Newton's Law of Universal Gravitation has survived very well for more than 300 years. It is still considered correct today within certain limits and it is widely used for problems involving falling objects and the motion of satellites around the earth.

Over the years, however, scientists began to notice that it was not accurate for all cases. The orbit of Mercury, the planet closest to the sun, doesn't quite follow the predicted path and nothing in Newton's science explains its behavior. Also, as more was learned about the speed of light, it became apparent that something important was missing from Newton's formula. There was no element of time.

Not having time in the formula means either that gravity never changes or that, if it does, it changes everywhere in the universe instantaneously. To use an unlikely example, imagine that our sun somehow suddenly vanished. Since light takes a little over eight minutes to travel from the sun to the earth, we wouldn't know the sun was gone until eight minutes later.

If the sun's mass suddenly disappeared, the force of gravity holding earth in its orbit would also be gone. Would this happen instantly or would it happen eight minutes later,

40

when the light went out? Newton's law says that it must happen instantly and not just to earth. The change must be felt everywhere in the universe at the same time.

EINSTEIN AND THE THEORY OF RELATIVITY

The idea of gravity traveling across the universe instantly bothered a young German scientist named Albert Einstein. Einstein had published a scientific paper in 1905 on the speed of light. Einstein reasoned that gravitation could travel no faster than light. Newton's law needed to be changed. Einstein published his ideas in their final form in 1916 in a paper called the "The Foundation of the General Theory of Relativity."

Einstein's theory is based on the dual property of matter mentioned earlier. Mass and force are related in two ways: by the attraction of gravity and by the resistance to acceleration. Einstein's theory says these two properties of mass are actually the same.

If you were accelerating through space in a rocket ship, for example, there is no measurement of force you could make that could tell the difference between the force caused by acceleration and a gravitational force of the same strength. Einstein called this principle *equivalence*.

Einstein's mathematics agree with Newton's for the smaller mass and weaker gravity that we find on earth. The two theories become different for the much larger mass and stronger gravity of the stars and our sun. Because Mercury is the closest planet to the sun, its orbit is affected by the sun's gravity in ways that aren't seen in the orbits of the other, more distant planets. Mercury's behavior is not explained by Newton's mathematics, but is by Einstein's.

Because all of our personal experience is with the weaker gravity of earth, we are much more comfortable with Newton's description of the universe. Einstein's universe contains dimensions and bizarre effects that are so far outside our experience they are difficult for us to imagine. They are even difficult for scientists and mathematicians to imagine or to describe in any terms except mathematical.

Among the strange predictions that come out of Einstein's theory are that time is slowed and space is curved by the presence of mass. Light travels in a curved path rather than in a straight line.

Many observations have been made over the years that show his predictions were correct. The bending of light rays was first seen by astronomers in 1919 as an apparent shift in the position of stars whose light passed very close to the sun.

More recently, astronomers have discovered several *gravitational lenses* far outside our galaxy. A gravitational "lens" is formed when light from a distant source is bent so much by a large mass that two separate images are seen from earth.

TOWARD A TEN-DIMENSIONAL UNIVERSE

Research into gravitation has not stopped with Einstein. Scientists are attempting to discover a formula and theory that will link the force of gravitation with the other fundamental forces to find a single unified theory of forces. Among the most promising current research is a strange

42

mathematical theory called *superstrings* that describes a ten-dimensional universe.

We are familiar with four dimensions: three dimensions of space or distance (length, width, and height) and one of time. In the ten-dimensional universe of superstrings, the particles of matter that we experience in our three dimensions as tiny points may actually be long "strings" in other dimensions.

Only much more research will tell if superstring theory gives the best description of our universe. It is likely that Nature still has many startling secrets hidden away to challenge our understanding. The main limits to further advances in gravitation research may well be the limits of our own imaginations.

4

Why Boats Float and Balloons Rise: Buoyancy

If you drop a brick and a block of wood into water, you know what will happen. The brick will sink and the wood will float. Why, exactly, does this happen? From a lifetime of experience with things that sink or float, we feel that it must have something to do with weight. The brick sinks because it is heavy and the wood floats because it is light.

Weight is part of the reason, but there is much more to sinking or floating than just weight. Enormously heavy steel ships float very well and relatively light wooden ones sometimes sink. What, then, really controls floating or sinking? The answer begins with our familiar force of gravity.

Boats float on the water, and helium and hot-air balloons rise in the air because of earth's gravity. It may seem strange that a force that pulls everything downward somehow pushes some things up. Yet, in liquids and gases, this is what happens.

Gravity pulls the liquid or gas surrounding an object down and that creates an upward force. This force can be so great that it is able to push a ship weighing millions of kilograms to the top of the water and push balloons thousands of meters up into the air. This upward force is known as *buoyancy*.

PRESSURE AND DEPTH IN LIQUIDS

Pour a little water into a glass, then tip the glass and watch the movement of the water. It will always stay as low as possible in the glass. It is almost as though all of the water molecules were fighting to get as close to the bottom as they can. In a sense, that is exactly what is happening. The weight of each water molecule pulls it downward toward the center of the earth. Since the molecules are free to move around each other, the water molds itself to match the shape of its container.

The weight of all these molecules pressing downward creates pressure. The deeper the water, the more water molecules there are pressing down from above and the greater the pressure. Have you ever dived to the bottom of a swimming pool? If you have, you know that the deeper you go, the greater the pressure you feel on your ears. It is this steady change in pressure with depth (called a pressure *gradient*) that creates the force of buoyancy.

You can do an experiment to see the effects of the pressure gradient in water. Take an empty aluminum soft-drink can and punch three holes in its side with a nail or other sharp tool. Punch one of the holes near the bottom of the can, one near the middle, and one near the top.

Then hold the open top of the can under a water faucet and turn on the water. Adjust the flow of water so it just keeps the can filled. Look at the streams of water flowing

Gravity causes an increase in water pressure with depth. You can see the effects of this pressure gradient by punching holes in the side of an aluminum can and filling it with water. The greater pressure causes the stream from the bottom hole to shoot farthest from the can.

out the punched holes. The higher pressure near the bottom of the can causes the stream from the bottom hole to shoot strongly while the stream from the middle hole is weaker and the one from the top hole is weakest of all.

This pressure gradient gives the buoyant force direction. It acts to move objects away from higher pressure and toward lower pressure. Remember that a pressure against an area, such as the sides, top, and bottom of an object, create force (Force = Pressure × Area). A higher pressure below an object than above means a greater force pushing upward than downward.

We live all of our lives in the pull of gravity, so we are used to liquids and gases always having a greater pressure with depth. It seems only natural that some things float and others sink. But if we were in a spaceship in orbit, where the pull of gravity is canceled out, the words "float" and "sink" would have no meaning.

In orbit, a block of wood inside a container of water would just hang suspended in the water. A helium-filled balloon in the cabin of a spaceship would just stay suspended in air. The pressure is the same in every part of the cabin. There is no gradient to force movement in any direction.

VOLUME, WEIGHT, AND DISPLACEMENT

Try putting a brick or stone or some other heavy, sinkable object into a bucket or sink of water and notice what happens to the water level. As the brick enters the water, the level of the water in the bucket rises. The brick is pushing aside some of the water. The word for this "pushing aside" of water is *displacement*. The brick *displaces* some of the water.

There are two important things about the amount of water that the brick displaced: its volume and its weight. The volume of the water that is displaced is exactly the same as the volume of the brick under water. If you could somehow catch the water displaced by the brick, you would find it would fill a container exactly the same size as the brick.

One way to catch the displaced water would be to start with a bucket filled to the very top rim. Then when you put

47

the brick in, all the displaced water would run over the side where it could be caught in another bucket below or perhaps in a larger bucket or tub containing the first bucket. Not easy to do without making quite a mess. Don't try this inside the house.

There is a connection between the weight of the displaced water and the weight of the brick. Bricks are quite heavy in air. What about in water? If you had some way of weighing the brick under water (perhaps with a hanging scales), you would find it is lighter in water than in air. It is lighter because the buoyant force of the water is pushing upward against the force of gravity.

The difference in the weight of the brick between air and water is equal to the *buoyant force*. (Actually, the brick has a tiny buoyant force in air, but the bucket of water does also, so we can forget about it.) How much lighter does the buoyant force make the brick?

If you could measure the weight of the water that was displaced, you would find that the brick was lighter by exactly that amount. In other words, the weight of the brick in air minus its weight in water is equal to the weight of the displaced water, and this force is the buoyant force. Let's see what would happen if the buoyant force were stronger.

What if the buoyant force was exactly the same as the weight of the brick in air? Then the weight of the brick in the water would be zero. With no weight, the brick wouldn't sink to the bottom. If it were exactly zero, the brick would just stay suspended in the water.

What if the buoyant force was much greater than the weight of the brick? Then the brick would be pushed up and part of it would stick up out of the water. With only

48

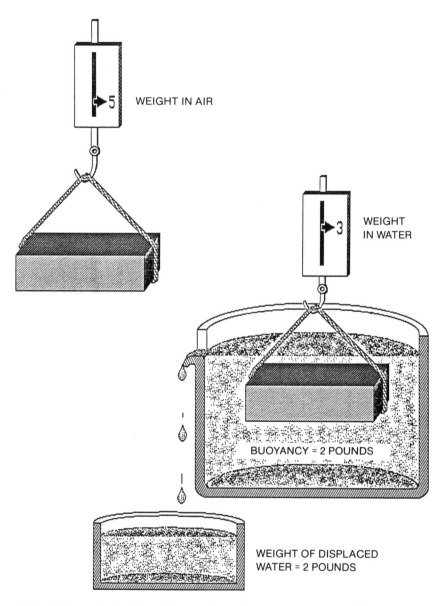

WEIGHT IN AIR

WEIGHT IN WATER

BUOYANCY = 2 POUNDS

WEIGHT OF DISPLACED WATER = 2 POUNDS

A brick that weighs about 5 pounds in air weighs about 3 pounds under water. When put into water, a brick displaces about 2 pounds of water—exactly the force of buoyancy pushing up on the brick. This is an example of Archimedes' principle.

part of the brick under water, the volume of water that was displaced would be less. With less water displaced, the buoyant force would then be less. The brick would float at a level where the two opposing forces exactly balanced. The buoyant force would exactly equal the weight of the brick.

You can feel the buoyant force for yourself. Take something that is light and filled with air, such as a ball or a plastic toy boat and put it into the water. Now press down on the ball and force it lower in the water. Feel the buoyant force pushing back? Watch the water level and notice the connection between the strength of the force and the height of the water. The more water that is displaced, the greater the buoyant force.

DENSITY

The strength of the buoyant force is decided by the weight of the volume of water that is displaced. There is a special word for the weight of a material in a certain volume. This is the *density*.

There are two kinds of density: weight density and mass density. With buoyancy, we are just interested in weight density. (The weight density of an object is its weight divided by its volume. It is the weight per each unit of volume.)

Materials such as iron or lead or brick have a high density. Materials such as cotton or feathers or a light wood have a low density. Whether an object sinks or floats depends upon its density compared with the density of water.

A brick sinks because the density of the brick material is greater than the density of water. Its weight for that volume is greater than the weight of the same volume of water.

ARCHIMEDES' PRINCIPLE

About 2,200 years ago, a Greek named Archimedes was said to have been given the problem of discovering if a crown made for the king was really made of pure gold and not of gold mixed with some cheaper metal. A way of finding out is said to have come to Archimedes as he lowered himself into a full bathtub.

He felt his weight become lighter in the water from buoyancy and he saw the water his body displaced overflow. He was so excited at his discovery, that he ran into the street without his clothes on shouting, "Eureka, eureka!" ("I have found it, I have found it!" in Greek).

Archimedes knew that gold is more dense than other metals and he used this to find the answer. He probably first had a block of pure gold made that was exactly the same weight as the crown. He could then use the amount of water displaced by each one to compare their volumes.

The crown was found to displace more water (to have a greater volume) than the pure gold. So, being the same weight, the crown was less dense than pure gold. The king had been tricked.

If Archimedes had had an accurate scales that worked in water as well as air, he could have tested the crown another way. Starting with the crown and a block of pure gold of the same weight in air, he could have then put them into water and again measured their weight. He would have discovered the crown to be lighter in water than the pure gold.

The principle of buoyancy is known today as Archimedes' principle. Archimedes' principle says that any object placed

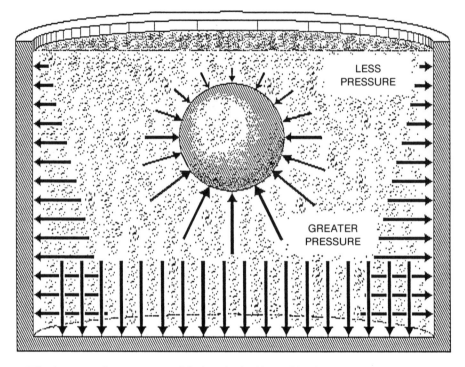

The increase in pressure with depth (indicated by longer arrows) creates a greater force on the bottom of an object than on its top. The difference between these top and bottom forces is the upward force known as *buoyancy*, the basis for Archimedes' principle.

in a liquid will become lighter by an amount that is the same as the weight of the liquid displaced. Since the crown displaced a greater amount of water than the pure gold, it would have been lighter in water than the gold.

STEEL SHIPS AND SUBMARINES

For a steel ship to float, it must be less dense than water. Steel is much more dense than water, but a ship is not solid steel. It has air inside. It is the overall or average density of an object, including the air inside, that decides whether it will sink or float.

The average density is the weight divided by the total volume of the ship. The average density of a huge ocean liner is much less than that of water, even though the density of the steel hull of the ship itself is much greater.

Submarines control the balance between weight and buoyancy by controlling their average density. When the crew of a submarine wants to submerge, they let water into tanks inside the hull, making the submarine's weight greater. Letting water in increases the average density of the submarine until it is greater than that of water. The same thing happens when water leaks inside a ship and causes it to sink.

Diving in a submarine must be done carefully because water is almost incompressible. It has almost the same density, no matter how great the pressure, and this keeps the buoyant force the same. Once a submarine or any other object sinks below the surface, there will be almost no increase in force to bring it back up and it will sink to the bottom no matter how deep the water. To keep this from happening, submarines use the power of their propellers and adjustments of their control planes to make up for small differences between weight and buoyancy.

FLOATING ON AIR

Buoyancy works almost the same in gases as in liquids. For a balloon in air, the weight of the air molecules creates an upward buoyant force on the balloon. If the gas inside the balloon is less dense than air, then the balloon will rise.

Buoyancy in air is different than in water because the density of the air is different at different altitudes. At low altitude, the greater pressure squeezes more air molecules together. The greater number of molecules in a volume gives a greater density. At high altitude, where the pressure is lower, the air is less dense.

Because of this, a balloon that rises from low altitude will not keep rising to the top of the atmosphere. It will rise only until the average density of the balloon and its cargo matches the density of the outside air and then it will stay suspended. This change in density makes the altitude of a balloon easier to control than the depth of a submarine.

We live out our lives under constant pressure caused by gravity. Buoyancy is only one of the effects of this pressure. In the next chapter, we will investigate some of the others, including some strange ones, such as its power to make water climb over the side of its container.

5

Atmospheric Pressure in Liquids and Gases

We live under enormous pressure. The weight of more than 200 kilometers (124 miles) of air in the atmosphere above presses down upon us. In terms of force, there is the weight of about 9,000 kilograms (20,000 pounds) spread over the area of your body, or about the weight of six automobiles.

We scarcely notice this pressure because our bodies are made for it. Our body cells are largely filled with water so they don't compress. Our lungs are something like a paper bag or balloon filled with air. They don't burst because the pressure inside our lungs is almost the same as outside. We could stand far greater pressures as long as the difference between inside and outside pressure stayed small.

This gravity-made pressure of the atmosphere is responsible for many strange and useful things. Besides making it possible for us to breathe, we use it for such everyday jobs as pushing milk or a soft drink into our mouths and cleaning our carpets. To see something of its power to push liquid, try the following experiment.

PUSHING WATER AROUND

Put a water glass or empty soft drink bottle into a sink or large bowl of water. Push it completely under water and turn the open end slightly up so that all the air inside the glass escapes. Then, turn the glass upside down, keeping the open end under the water. Now lift the glass up until only the open end is under the water. What happens to the water inside the glass?

It may seem strange, but the water doesn't run out. Something keeps it up inside the glass. That "something" is atmospheric pressure. The pressure of the air pushes down on the surface of the water outside and holds the water up in the glass. Because you let the air out of the glass, there is no opposing air pressure to keep the water down. It is forced up into the glass against the force of gravity.

When you drink through a straw, it seems as though you are pulling the liquid up into your mouth. That is not exactly what happens. It is more accurate to say that the liquid is being pushed into your mouth. It is being pushed from a higher pressure to a lower pressure area.

When you drink, your tongue and the muscles of your cheeks and jaw move to create a space inside your mouth that has a larger volume and a lower air pressure than the outside air. Your lips make a tight seal around the end of the straw so no air can leak in to balance the pressure. The higher pressure of the air then pushes down on the surface of the liquid and it flows up the straw and into your mouth.

A vacuum cleaner works much the same way. A powerful electric fan creates a low pressure inside the vacuum cleaner. The higher pressure air from outside rushes in and carries

Turn a glass upside down in a sink of water, lift it up, and atmospheric pressure will hold the water inside the glass. This toy diver floats up inside the glass with the help of a plastic bag of air attached to his back.

dirt from the carpet with it. A filter in the cleaner traps the dirt but allows the air to pass through.

MAKING ZERO PRESSURE

The pressure of the atmosphere is strong enough to push a column of water up inside a glass, even though water is quite heavy. Is there any limit to how high water can be pushed? Instead of a drinking glass, imagine a very tall glass tube filled with water. This tube is closed on the top end like the glass and has an open bottom end that is under water in a full sink or bowl.

If we kept making the tube taller and taller, we would discover that the water would stay up inside the tube up to a level of about 10.33 meters (33 feet 11 inches) above the surface of the water in the sink or bowl. After that, no matter how much taller you make the tube, the water level would reach no higher. This limit is related to the change in water pressure with depth.

The pressure at the surface of the water is that of the atmosphere. Air pressure pushes on the surface of the water just as it does on everything else. (In the metric system it is about 10.1 newtons per square centimeter. In the English system, this pressure is about 14.7 pounds per square inch.)

If you went below the surface of the water, the pressure would become greater. If you went up inside the tube, above the surface of the water, the pressure will be less. What happens when you finally reach zero pressure?

The water stops there. No more water can be above you or the pressure wouldn't be zero. This level where the water stops is about 10.33 meters above the surface. What lies above this level? Nothing. At least, almost nothing. You have created a near vacuum.

It isn't a perfect vacuum because it does contain a little water vapor (water in the form of a gas), but it is close enough that you couldn't survive there, even with a tank of air to breathe. Our lungs are designed for pressure, but we can't put pressure inside them without a nearly balancing pressure around us. Like a balloon inflated with too much air, our lungs would burst. We would have to have a completely pressurized suit such as astronauts have to survive.

THE BAROMETER AND *HORROR VACUI*

The pressure of the air pushes water up in the tube. The weight of the water in the tube above the surface level exactly matches the opposing force caused by atmospheric pressure. What would you expect to happen if atmospheric pressure became less? A lower pressure would not support as great a weight of water and the column of liquid would sink lower in the tube.

This was first observed by Evangelista Torricelli in Italy in about 1643. Instead of water, Torricelli used the liquid metal, mercury. Mercury is over 13 times more dense than water. Instead of reaching 10.33 meters, a column of mercury reaches only about 76 centimeters (30 inches). The changes in the height of the column of mercury, Torricelli said, ". . . shows the mutations of the air, now heavier and dense, and now lighter and thin."

Torricelli's invention is called a *barometer*. Barometers are valuable instruments to meteorologists in their study of the

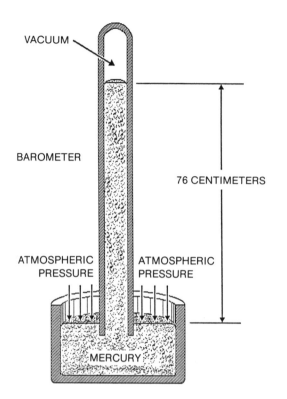

VACUUM

BAROMETER

76 CENTIMETERS

ATMOSPHERIC PRESSURE   ATMOSPHERIC PRESSURE

MERCURY

The first barometer for measuring atmospheric pressure was made in about 1643, using a glass tube of mercury above a dish. At that time, the vacuum in the tube above the mercury created a greater sensation than the barometer.

weather. Another use for the barometer was found shortly after its invention. After hearing of Torricelli's invention, the French scientist and mathematician, Blaise Pascal, built one for himself using red wine instead of mercury. Pascal wanted to know if air pressure became less at higher altitudes.

Pascal first tried taking the instrument up to the top of a church tower, but the change in pressure was too small to measure. Pascal then had his brother-in-law carry a barometer to the top of a mountain. There he measured a difference in height of the liquid of nearly 8 centimeters (3 inches) from its height at the bottom of the mountain. What had only been a theory was now proven: air pressure changes with altitude.

When the discovery of the barometer became known, there was great excitement throughout Europe. Not because of its ability to measure pressure, but because of the vacuum above the liquid. Until Torricelli's and Pascal's time, a vacuum was almost unimaginable. Aristotle had believed that Nature had a horror for any empty space (*horror vacui* in Latin) and would not permit a vacuum to be formed.

Around 1650, a German named Otto von Guericke invented an air pump that could pump most of the air out of a sealed container. People marveled at experiments in which mice died, candles were put out, and bells became silent when the air was pumped out of their container.

In a famous experiment, von Guericke demonstrated the enormous force of atmospheric pressure by creating a vacuum inside a two-piece hollow metal ball. When the air had been pumped out, two teams of horses pulling in opposite directions on the two halves of the ball could not pull it apart.

THE SIPHON: MAKING WATER RUN UPHILL

The gravity-caused pressure on air and water has another useful, almost magical ability. It can make water run up hill (as long as the "hill" is less than 10.33 meters above the surface of the water in the container). We can do this with a simple device known as a *siphon*.

A siphon is a kind of pump that carries liquid up over the side of a container and down to a lower level. You have probably used siphons all of your life without realizing it. The most common use of a siphon is in the home toilet.

You can make a siphon very easily. You will need a bucket

or other large container for the water and a tube or hose about a meter (about 3 feet) long. A piece of old garden hose is ideal.

Fill the bucket with water and put the hose into the bucket. Hold it completely under and try to get all of the air bubbles out. Then close off one end of the hose by putting your finger over the hole.

Quickly lift the closed end of the tube over the side of the bucket and hang it down over the side, below the level of the water in the bucket. Now let go of the closed end of the tube and you should see water start to flow.

The water really climbs up over the side of the bucket. It will keep flowing until the water in the bucket is gone or until the level of the water in the bucket reaches the same level as water coming out of the hose. Experiment with raising the lower end of the hose. You will find the siphon stops flowing the instant the lower end is raised to the same level or higher than the surface level of the water in the bucket.

If you had a siphon going between two containers on different levels, water would flow from the upper one into the lower one. If you raised the lower one, the water would flow back in the other direction. You have just made an efficient pump that is able to pump almost any amount of water, that has no moving parts, and that doesn't need batteries. Gravity provides the power.

MYSTERIES OF THE SIPHON REVEALED

A siphon works by pressure difference. For the siphon to pump, the hose outside the bucket must be longer than the

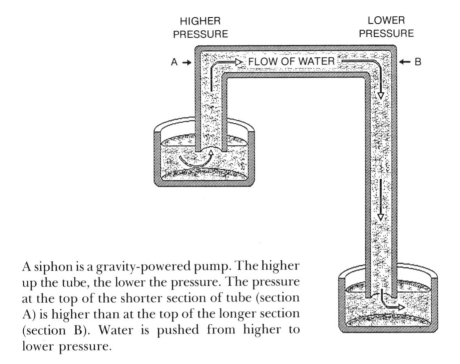

HIGHER PRESSURE   LOWER PRESSURE

A → FLOW OF WATER ← B

A siphon is a gravity-powered pump. The higher up the tube, the lower the pressure. The pressure at the top of the shorter section of tube (section A) is higher than at the top of the longer section (section B). Water is pushed from higher to lower pressure.

hose inside the bucket (actually, not the hose itself, but the distance measured straight down from the highest point at the bend in the hose to the surface of the water).

Because the height of the water in the hose inside the bucket is less, the pressure in the part of the hose inside the bucket is greater at the top than the pressure in the longer, outside part of the hose. This pressure difference pushes the water through the hose, just as a pressure difference pushes liquid through a drinking straw and into your mouth.

There are some clues in these pressures that tell about the conditions needed for a siphon to work. First, a siphon can only transfer liquid to a lower level. Siphons don't really pump water uphill. At least, the final level that they pump to can't be higher than the starting level. If the levels become the same, there is no pressure difference and there will be no more flow.

For example, a siphon wouldn't work under water. There would be no difference in pressure. You could, however, siphon some liquid with a greater density than water. For example, mercury could be siphoned under water.

A siphon needs five conditions to work: (1) there must be pressure, (2) the pressure must change with distance, (3) there must be two different liquids or gases with different weight densities, (4) the end of the hose outside must be lower than the surface level inside the container, and (5) the top of the siphon can be no higher than the zero pressure level for that liquid.

HOW TOILETS REALLY WORK

Have you ever wondered what makes a toilet flush? You push the handle down, water starts to pour down into the bowl from the tank at the back, and then, suddenly, most of the water in the bottom of the toilet bowl is mysteriously pulled out of the bowl and disappears down the drain. The standard home toilet is a simple, but very clever, design that puts the siphon to practical use.

The pipe at the bottom of a toilet bowl is shaped something like an "S" lying on its side. The entrance to this pipe is the opening in the bottom of the bowl. The rest of the "S" is out of sight behind the bowl. The siphon works to pull the water in the bowl up and over the curve of this "S"-shaped pipe.

When a toilet is not being flushed, the water level in the bowl is just up to the lower edge of the "S" pipe. The water

64

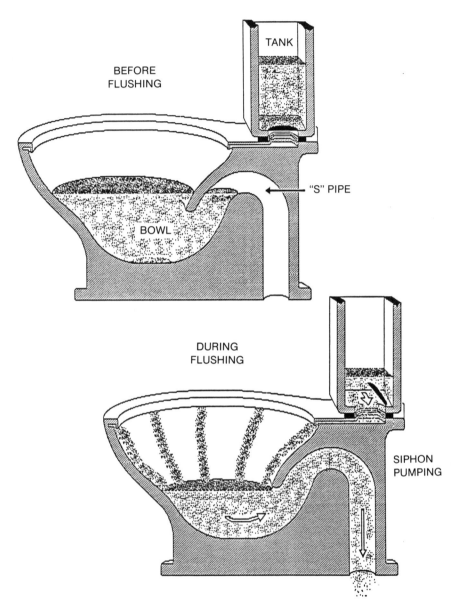

BEFORE
FLUSHING

TANK

"S" PIPE

BOWL

DURING
FLUSHING

SIPHON
PUMPING

Most toilets use siphon pumping. When flushed, water from the tank above pours down, causing the level in the bowl to rise until it fills the "S"-shaped pipe behind the bowl. Siphon pumping then pulls water from the bowl until air enters, which stops the flushing.

in the bowl blocks any odors from coming up from the drain pipe. No water is flowing because the upper part of the "S"-pipe siphon is filled with air.

Pressing the handle down to flush the toilet opens a valve in the water tank above the toilet. The water starts to pour down into the bowl through small holes around the sides. This new water raises the level of the water in the bowl and water starts to pour over the top of the "S" and down the drain.

If the water level in the bowl rises fast enough, the "S" will be filled with water and the siphon pumping will begin. Once the siphon is started, it will keep on pumping until the bowl is emptied and air is pulled in. As soon as air is in the pipe, the siphon action is broken and the pumping stops. The bowl then slowly fills back to its original level.

Science can be found at work even in places as humble as a toilet, but only if you know what to look for. While not too many people are interested in the toilets themselves, there is something to be learned from the ideas of how they work. Sometimes the simplest ideas are the most ingenious of all.

Gravity and the gravity-caused forces that we have seen so far have been *static,* that is, they exist without any motion. The next force we will investigate is *dynamic,* that is, it is created by motion. This is the force that makes airplanes fly.

6

How Airplanes Fly: The Force of Lift

If you jump from a high place, you are not too surprised when you fall straight to the ground. You know that "thin air" won't hold you up. You can float on water. The force of buoyancy in water is great enough to hold you up. But air is nearly 800 times less dense than water. It takes a helium or hot-air balloon the size of a small house to lift a person's weight into the air.

But "thin" air does have the ability to support enormous weight. A Boeing 747 jetliner, for example, weighs about 326,000 kilograms (720,000 pounds) and is able to carry more than 350 people and their luggage to heights of more than 10,000 meters (33,000 feet). This is more weight than could be lifted by any balloon, blimp, or dirigible ever made.

The force that holds up a heavier-than-air craft like a jetliner is completely different from the buoyant force that holds up a balloon. Buoyancy doesn't need any motion. The force that holds up aircraft is created with motion. Take away motion and it disappears. This force is the force of *lift*.

67

BERNOULLI'S PRINCIPLE

This force was first described mathematically in 1738 by the Swiss scientist and mathematician, Daniel Bernoulli. While experimenting with liquids flowing through pipes, Bernoulli discovered a strange thing. He found that the pressure of the liquid on the sides of the pipe became less as the speed of flow through the pipe became greater.

The relationship between speed of flow and the side pressure is known today as Bernoulli's principle. Bernoulli's experiments were with liquids, but his basic principle also holds for gases. Bernoulli's principle describes a force that is at right angles (sideways) to the direction of flow. And this force becomes less as the speed of flow becomes faster. You can do a simple experiment with Bernoulli's principal, using two sheets of paper, such as notebook paper or typing paper.

Hold the edges of two pieces of paper flat together, one in each hand, and bow the center of the sheets apart to form a sort of tube. Now put one end of the "tube" up to your mouth and blow a strong stream of air through the center between the pieces of paper. If the air stream is strong enough, the tube will collapse as the two sheets of paper try to come together.

This is contrary to what our experience might tell us should happen. From experience inflating balloons, we expect the walls of the tube to be forced out rather than inward. The high-speed air that you forced through the middle created a side pressure on the paper walls that was lower than the pressure of the still air outside the paper tube. This difference in pressure over the area of the paper

Lift is the side pressure made by the flow of a liquid or gas past a solid surface. The faster the flow, the lower the side pressure. If you blow a stream of air through a "tube" made of two pieces of paper, the lower pressure created by the air flow will cause the paper tube to collapse.

made a force strong enough to push the sheets of paper inward.

THE FORCE OF LIFT

The force of lift is caused by pressure difference on a surface area, such as the wings of an aircraft. To create an upward force, there must be a lower pressure on top of a wing and a higher pressure below. The amount of lift on a wing is controlled by three things: (1) the speed of the air flow over the wing, (2) the size and shape of the wing, and (3) the angle of attack of the wing.

The flow of air over a wing causes lift. It doesn't matter if the wing is standing still and the air is moving or if the wing is moving and the air is still. It is only the relative movement of the air over the wing that is important.

The next time you see an airplane, notice the shape of its wings. A view of the end of one of the wings is best. Notice that the wings are curved, not flat, and that the top of the wing has a greater curve than the bottom. The curved shape of a wing helps it create lift.

As air flows around a wing, the air separates into two

Airplane wings are more curved on top than below to give them greater lift. The *Spirit of St. Louis,* on display in the Smithsonian Institution in Washington, D.C., carried Charles Lindbergh on the first solo flight across the Atlantic in May, 1927.

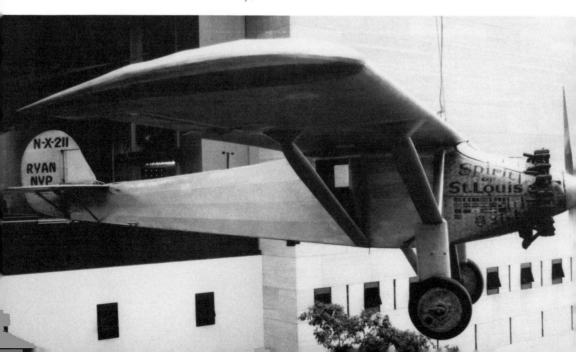

streams, one that flows over the top of the wing and one that flows below. Because the top of the wing is larger and more rounded than the bottom, the air flowing over the top must travel a greater distance before it comes together again with the air over the lower part of the wing.

Because it travels a longer distance in the same time, the speed of the air over the top of the wing is slightly greater than the speed of the air below the wing. A greater speed, according to Bernoulli's principle, means a lower pressure. A pressure difference with a lower pressure on top and a greater pressure below creates the net upward force of lift on the wing.

The lift of a wing can be increased by tilting it upward at an angle to the air flow. This gives the wing a greater *angle of attack*. There is an angle of attack (usually about 18 degrees) at which lift is greatest. If the angle of attack is made too large, the air will no longer flow smoothly over the wing and lift will become less.

THE FORCE OF DRAG

There is another force acting on a wing from the flow of air. This is the force of *drag*. As the name indicates, drag acts to slow the speed of the wing through the air. If there were no drag, an aircraft could just keep going faster and faster. A flat wing, such as you might make for a paper airplane, can create lift if given some angle of attack, but it will have greater drag for the same amount of lift than a properly curved wing.

Aircraft designers try to create wing shapes with a large amount of lift, but with as little drag as possible. Orville and

The Wright brothers experimented with over 200 different wing designs trying to find a shape that gave the greatest lift for the least drag. Their Wright *Flyer*, on display at the Smithsonian, made the first successful powered flight on December 17, 1903.

Wilbur Wright, who flew the first successful powered aircraft on December 17, 1903, experimented with over 200 different wing shapes, trying to find a design that gave the greatest lift for the least drag. It is a quest that still goes on today. Aircraft engineers continue to experiment with different shapes in wind tunnels and by computer analysis.

72

CONTROLLED FLIGHT

One of the reasons that the Wright brothers succeeded in flying where others failed was because they realized that the main problem of flight is control. Controlling an aircraft involves controlling one or more of the three things that cause lift: the speed of air flow, the size or shape of the wings or control surfaces, and the angle of attack.

BREAKING THE SOUND BARRIER

Advances in design and materials have created aircraft capable of faster and faster speeds. During World War II, aircraft would sometimes develop control problems in a high-speed dive. There seemed to be a kind of barrier to further increases in speed. This speed "limit" was at the same speed that sound travels through the air and came to be known as the *sound barrier.*

Have you ever wondered why there is a connection between how fast sound travels and the flight of a high-speed aircraft? Sound is something that we hear. It doesn't seem to have anything at all to do with flight. As we will find in the next chapter, it is not the sound itself, but the way that sound is carried from one place to another that affects the flight of aircraft.

1

Traveling Waves of Pressure: Sound

When anything moves or vibrates in the air, waves of pressure travel outward in all directions at high speed. Sensors on the sides of your head detect these pressure waves and send signals about them to your brain. Your brain recognizes patterns to these waves and often finds meaning in them. These traveling waves of pressure are sound waves and the forces they transmit to your ear "sensors" carry valuable information about the world around you.

The speech of friends, the rhythms of music, and the warning sound of approaching cars on the street are only a few examples of the information carried by sound. The ability to hear these sounds is one of our most important senses, perhaps second only to our sense of sight.

Sound always starts with motion. Something must move to disturb the air. The sounds of a piano, for example, are made by taut strings (actually wires) vibrating rapidly back and forth. Your voice comes from the vibration of the vocal cords in your throat. Touch your fingers to your throat while you speak and you can feel the vibrations.

74

Sound is caused by a disturbance of the air. The back and forth vibrations of a string on this Autoharp cause waves of high- and low-pressure air to travel outward in all directions.

CONNECTING FORCE TO THE AIR

Any movement or vibration requires force. Force is transmitted to the air as pressure. A piano string that has been struck vibrates back and forth, changing the pressure of the air next to the string. When the string moves out, the air next to it is compressed slightly, so there is a small increase in the air pressure there. Energy is transferred from the string to the air in this raised pressure.

This increased pressure next to the piano string pushes the air molecules closer together so that they collide with other molecules more often than they did at the lower pressure. These tiny collisions between billions of molecules act something like speeding marbles striking other marbles and they, in turn, moving and striking yet others.

The result of all these molecular collisions is that the area of increased pressure moves outward from the string in a circular "wave," much like the way ripples travel out in circles from a stone dropped into a pool of water. As the wave front becomes a larger and larger circle (actually, a ball-like sphere because it is in three dimensions), the pressure is spread over an ever-greater area. The pressure at any one place, such as your eardrum, becomes less and less the farther you are away from the source of the sound.

When the string moves back in the other direction, it creates a low pressure area that will travel along behind the high one. The back-and-forth vibrations make a series of high and low pressure waves that travel out in ever-widening circles. The original molecules of air that were at the start of this wave don't keep traveling with it. They move only enough to pass their energy on to other molecules next to them.

When these waves of high and low pressure strike the thin skin membrane of your eardrum, the pressure changes on the area of the eardrum create a force that moves the eardrum back and forth at exactly the same rate that the piano string moved. By carrying the patterns of the string motion in the form of pressure waves, the air connects your ears to the piano strings.

76

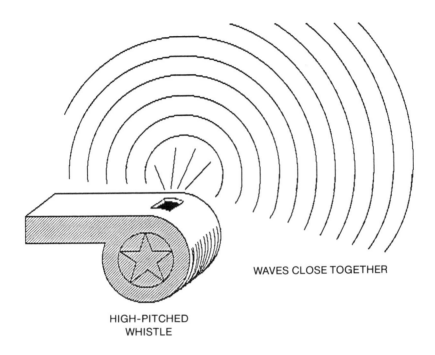

WAVES CLOSE TOGETHER

HIGH-PITCHED
WHISTLE

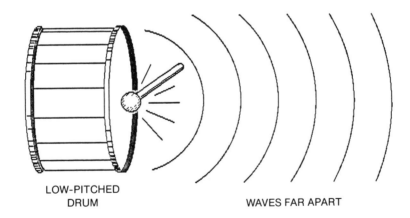

LOW-PITCHED
DRUM

WAVES FAR APART

The pressure waves of a high-pitched sound such as a whistle are close together in time and distance. The waves of a low-pitched sound, such as a drum, are farther apart.

77

A SOUND MEDIUM

Because sound travels by collisions between molecules, there must be molecules of matter present or there can be no sound. Sound requires a *medium*. It needs some matter to carry it. We are most familiar with sound in air, but sound travels in every material.

A bell ringing inside a vacuum chamber is silent. There is no air to carry the sound to our ears. Science-fiction movies often show scenes with rocket ships emitting a roaring sound as they travel through space. Either the movie makers don't know, or else they think movie audiences don't know that real space is totally silent.

THE SPEED OF SOUND

Sound waves travel at very different speeds in different materials. The exact speed depends upon how elastic or flexible the material is, its density, its temperature, and its pressure.

For example, the speed of sound in air at sea level at 15 degrees Celsius (59 degrees Fahrenheit) and normal air pressure, is 340 meters (1,116 feet) per second. If the air temperature is hotter, the speed will be greater. At a burning hot 1,000 degrees Celsius, the speed is over twice as fast.

If you go up in altitude, where the pressure and temperature of the air are lower, the speed of sound is less than at sea level. At 10,000 meters, for example, the speed of sound is about 300 meters per second.

The speed of sound is usually faster in liquids than in gases. Liquids have two properties that act in opposite

78

directions on the speed of sound. Liquids are more dense than gases, and sound travels more slowly through materials with greater density. But liquids are also less elastic, less easy to compress and expand, and sound travels faster through materials that are less elastic.

In water, for example, these two opposing effects give sound a speed that is over four times as fast as the speed through air. The temperature of the water is also important. Cold water is more dense than warm water, and sound travels a little slower through cold water than through warm.

The speed of sound is faster in many solids than it is in liquids. The harder the material (the less elastic), the greater the speed. A material that has one of the fastest speeds is the stone known as granite. The speed of sound through granite is about 6,000 meters (19,685 feet) per second.

Among the slowest materials for sound is rubber, which is very elastic. Rubber carries sound at about 54 meters (177 feet) per second. This is about 120 miles or 200 kilometers per hour, about the top speed of a fast car.

Our most common experience with the speed of sound is usually with thunder during a storm. Have you ever seen a flash of lightning and then listened for the crash of thunder a few seconds later? The time spent waiting for the thunder was the difference in time between when the light reached your eyes and when the sound reached your ears. The speed of sound is very much slower than that of light. Light travels so fast (300,000 kilometers or 186,000 miles per second) that it seems instantaneous compared to sound.

You can find how far away a lightning strike was by measuring the time before you hear the thunder. It takes the sound about three seconds to travel one kilometer or about five seconds to travel one mile. To find the distance, count the number of seconds between the lightning flash and the sound of the thunder. Divide by three to find the distance in kilometers or by five to find it in miles.

SOUND REFLECTIONS

Have you ever heard an echo? An echo happens when sound waves reflect off a building or a canyon wall or some other large, hard object and bounce back to you. You shout and a second or two later you hear your voice back again. If you are between two walls, it is sometimes possible to get multiple echoes, where you hear your voice bounced back more than once.

Sound waves are reflected when they strike a different kind of material than the one they are traveling through. When sound traveling through air strikes a wall, for example, some of the sound penetrates the wall and keeps going, but most of the sound is reflected back. The amount that gets reflected depends upon the difference in speed in the other material. That is why hard materials such as stone and glass give the best echoes and soft materials such as curtains and carpets stop echoes.

Even when you can't hear a clear echo, you are still hearing sound reflected back from everything around you. If someone is talking to you, the sound you hear straight from that person gets mixed together with reflections of their voice from the walls, floor, ceiling, and other nearby objects. All of these reflections slightly change the way their voice sounds to your ears.

80

You use these reflections to tell you about the space around you, usually without being aware of it. Your voice or the sound of your footsteps or any other noise sounds different in a small room than it does outdoors or in a large auditorium, for example. Even blindfolded, you could tell a lot about where you were just from the way things sound. Try listening for these differences when you go to different places.

BENDING SOUND: REFRACTION

Besides reflection, sound waves can change their direction in still another way. Sound waves can be bent, or *refracted,* when they enter a material that transmits them at a different speed. This refraction of sound waves most often happens in air or in water when there are layers of different temperatures.

You may have noticed how much farther sound seems to carry above the water of a lake or river. Often there is a layer of cool air just over the water and warmer air above. Normally sound waves travel out in all directions. If you shout a warning to a friend some distance away, only a tiny part of the sound waves of your voice reach your friend's ears. Most are lost to the air above and to the sides.

With a warm layer of air above you, however, a part of the wave traveling upward will be bent back when it enters the warmer air. This adds to and strengthens the sound waves within the cool layer, so your friend will be able to hear your voice at a greater distance.

SOUND AND MOTION: THE DOPPLER EFFECT

You know how some sounds, like the sound of a whistle, have a high pitch and others, like that of a large bass drum, have a low pitch. The spacing of the waves in time sets the pitch or frequency of the sound. If the waves are close together in time, the sound will be a high-pitched note. If they are farther apart, it will have a low pitch.

The slowness of the speed of sound can make some interesting changes to the pitch that we hear when either the source of the sound or the receiver is moving. This apparent change in pitch caused by speed between the source of the sound and the receiver is called the *Doppler effect*. It was named after the Austrian physicist, Christian Doppler.

To understand how the Doppler effect works, imagine first that you are standing still listening to a friend blow on a whistle. The time between the waves of high pressure as they leave the whistle is the same as the time between the waves that strike your ear. The pitch that your friend hears and the pitch that you hear are the same.

Now imagine that you are in a car traveling toward your friend at high speed. The waves of sound are traveling at the same speed as before, but now you are moving toward the oncoming waves and so the time between the waves striking your ears is less than when you were standing still. To your ear, this sounds exactly as if the whistle were higher pitched. To your friend's ear, the whistle still sounds the same.

As you pass your friend, the pitch will drop and as you

travel away, the opposite effect happens. The pitch you hear will be lower than the pitch you heard while standing still. What if you were in a jet plane traveling at the same speed as sound?

AT SUPERSONIC SPEEDS

If you were traveling at exactly the speed of sound toward a source of sound, the pitch you would hear would be double that heard when standing still. If the pitch of the whistle was already high when standing still, the Doppler effect might push the pitch outside the range of human hearing.

As you passed the whistle, the pitch would become lower as before. But, instead of just dropping to a low pitch, it would drop to nothing. As you traveled away, there would be no sound from the whistle at all. The sound waves from the whistle would never pass your ear because you are traveling at the same speed they are.

Now imagine that you have the whistle instead of your friend. You are traveling toward your friend at the speed of sound as before. Now you blow on the whistle. Can your friend hear the whistle? The answer is no. You would pass your friend at the same time as the sound. Only then would your friend hear the whistle.

The sound of the whistle together with the sound of the jet carrying you and the disturbance made by its passage through the air would bunch up around and behind you as a powerful wave of pressure known as a shock wave. The shock wave behind a jet traveling at supersonic speeds

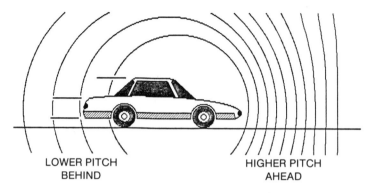

LOWER PITCH
BEHIND

HIGHER PITCH
AHEAD

Speed causes a change in pitch known as the Doppler effect. At speeds less than the speed of sound, the pitch is higher ahead of the moving object and lower behind. At supersonic speeds, there is no sound ahead of the aircraft. The sound waves behind form a triangular-shaped shock wave.

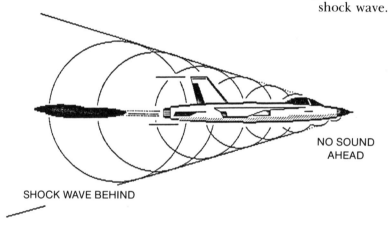

NO SOUND
AHEAD

SHOCK WAVE BEHIND

(speeds greater than that of sound) can be strong enough to break windows and damage homes if the plane is at low altitude.

SUPERSONIC FLIGHT

In the last chapter, we wondered about the connection between the speed of sound and the flight of aircraft. It is not sound as something that can be heard that affects aircraft. The connection lies with the nature of sound as a wave of pressure. Pressure affects the lift created by the wings and control surfaces.

An aircraft in flight has a balance of forces acting on it. The forces of lift and drag are caused by high and low pressures. As the speed of an aircraft nears the speed that a wave of pressure can move through the air, the locations of these high and low pressure areas on the aircraft change. Any change in the amount and the locations of pressure areas can create flight control problems.

In the mid-1940s, around the end of World War II, advances in aircraft and engine design made it possible for aircraft to reach supersonic speed in a dive. Planes sometimes crashed because they lost control and were not able to pull out of a dive. The pressure changes that happen around the speed of sound weren't understood then and aircraft were not designed to handle them. Today's supersonic jets are designed to pass through the sound barrier with only a slightly bumpy ride.

BEYOND MATTER

The forces we have investigated so far have been connected with matter in some way. In the next chapters, we will look at a pair of forces that are able to travel in a wave that behaves like a sound wave in some ways, but with several important differences. These forces are the fastest in the universe, and they travel best when there is no matter at all.

8

Electromagnetism:
The Magnetic Force

We don't usually think of ourselves as being held together by electricity. We don't feel very "electric," whatever that might be like. Electricity, for most of us, is something that comes out of a socket on the wall and lights our homes and powers our appliances. Yet, electricity is part of what holds ourselves and every other bit of matter in the universe together. The source of this universal "glue" is found within atoms themselves. This is the fundamental force known as *electromagnetism*.

As its name sounds, the electromagnetic force has a dual nature. It is formed from two different, but related forces: the *electric force* and the *magnetic force*. Until the early part of the last century, electricity and magnetism were studied as two separate sciences and no connection between them was known.

Almost by accident, it was discovered that a flow of electric current (a movement of electrical charge) creates a magnetic force. Some years later, a changing magnetic force was found to cause an electric current to flow in a wire. The connection between the electric force and the magnetic force was found to be in change or movement. Anytime there is movement or flow, both forces will be present.

Today, the two forces are studied as a single branch of science, but we still do many experiments with them in their separate, static forms. This chapter and the next will explore the magnetic and electric forces, first alone and then combined. Let's begin with the force of magnetism.

THE MAGNETIC FORCE

About 900 years ago, the Chinese began to use a mysterious force that seemed to be contained in certain kinds of rock. When held up by a string or placed on a piece of wood floating on water, a piece of this ore would turn itself to point toward the north. This ore, known today as magnetite or lodestone, is a natural permanent magnet. By making the piece of lodestone free to turn, they created a magnetic compass.

At that time, a magnet and the force it contained must have seemed like magic. Today, we have a more scientific understanding of magnets, but their power to attract or to repel with an invisible force field is still fascinating. (A magnetic "field" is any region where magnetic force is present.) Magnetic force is the invisible workhorse of the twentieth century, and there are magnetic fields almost everywhere we go today.

We are constantly surrounded by magnetic fields. In fact, we are constantly being sliced through by them. Their force passes through our bodies as if we weren't there and we have no sense of their presence. Nothing that we are able to see, hear, touch, taste, or smell gives us any hint that we are within a magnetic field. If we were somehow able to see these fields, we would discover bizarre sights wherever we went.

Besides the enormous field of the earth reaching far out into space, we would see rapidly changing magnetic fields swirling out of the walls from the electrical wiring in our home and from every electric motor. Magnetic fields cause

About 900 years ago, the Chinese began to use a mysterious force that we know today as *magnetism*. The magnetized needle of a compass aligns itself with the magnetic force field of the earth.

electric motors to turn. The refrigerator, the washing machine, the dryer, and the vacuum cleaner all have electric motors and we would see fields around all of them.

Television sets use a strong magnetic field to create the picture on the picture tube. A magnetic field is used to move the cone of the loudspeaker in a radio and the earphone in the telephone. There are so many magnetic fields everywhere around us, it is probably best that we are not able to see them. We would scarcely be able to see anything else.

MAGNETS AND MAGNETIC FIELDS

One of the interesting things about the magnetic force is that it can be created in several different ways. The two main ways are: (1) *ferromagnetism,* caused by the orientation or direction of certain kinds of atoms and, (2) *electromagnetism,* caused by passing an electric current through a conductor such as a metal wire. The magnetic field that is created by either method is exactly the same.

A magnetic field is always *polarized,* that is, its force has a direction that is set by the two *poles* of the magnet. Every magnet has two poles, usually called the "north" and "south" poles. Opposite poles attract each other (the north pole of one magnet pulls strongly toward the south pole of another magnet) and the same poles repel (the north pole of one magnet pushes away from the north pole of another magnet and, likewise, any two south poles repel).

Magnetic fields can both add and subtract. If two magnets are close together and pointing in the same direction, their fields add to make a total, stronger field. If the magnets are close together, but their poles facing in opposite directions, their fields oppose each other to give a very weak overall field.

A magnet must have both poles to have a magnetic field (to be a magnet, in other words). If we were to take a straight bar magnet, with the north pole on one end and the south pole on the other, and cut it in half, we would discover that we had created two new, separate magnets, each with its own north and south pole.

If we kept cutting a permanent magnet into smaller and smaller pieces (each a complete magnet itself), we would eventually reach a microscopic size where one last cut would kill the magnetic properties. The smallest possible magnet that can exist in a material is called a magnetic *domain*. A domain is a group of a million or so atoms of matter that have aligned themselves in the same direction to form a tiny magnet.

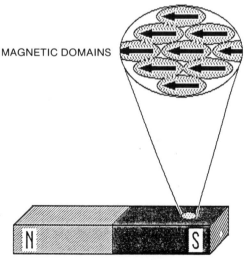

MAGNETIC DOMAINS

Permanent magnets created by ferromagnetism are formed when tiny *domains* made of millions of iron atoms are aligned in the same direction. These domains are invisible to the eye.

PERMANENT MAGNET

FERROMAGNETISM

Ferromagnetism is created by these domains. The prefix "ferro" comes from the Latin word for iron. Iron, nickel, and cobalt are the three main elements that have these magnetic domains. Ferromagnetism is also possible in certain rare earths and alloys.

In iron that is not magnetized, these domains point in all different directions. With all the tiny domains pointing in different directions, the sum of all their magnetic fields added together has no overall direction, so there is no polarity and no overall magnetic field.

If a piece of iron is placed in a strong magnetic field, say by touching or rubbing it against a magnet, the domains turn like microscopic compass needles to align themselves with the direction of the field. The stronger the magnetic field, the greater the number of domains that become aligned. The more domains that are aligned, the stronger the magnet will be.

If the magnetic field is taken away, the domains do not return to their random directions. They stay pointing in the direction they were set. With the domains pointing the same way, their fields add together to give the iron a net magnetic field. The iron is now magnetized and it will stay that way unless something happens to turn the domains back to their original conditions.

A MAGNETIC COMPASS

If you have a permanent magnet, such as the horseshoe-shaped kind found in toy stores or hardware or radio supply stores, try this experiment. Magnetize a paper clip or needle or other small piece of iron or steel by rubbing it against the magnet. (A pin won't work because pins are not made of steel.) You can test to see if it is magnetized by seeing if it will stick to other paper clips or needles.

When you are sure the paper clip is magnetized, fill a bowl with water and float the paper clip on a small "boat" of wooden match sticks or a piece of wooden popsicle stick. In fact, if you lower the paper clip into the water very

You can make a compass from a paper clip. Magnetize the clip by rubbing it against any magnet. Then float the clip in a bowl of water. The clip will turn to point north.

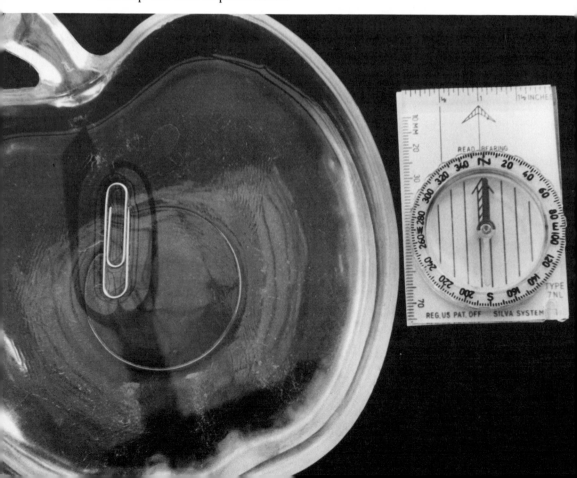

carefully with a fork, the surface of the water will support it without the "boat." This is caused by a strange force at the surface of the water that we will investigate in a later chapter.

It is very important that the bowl not be close to any metal when you do this. Any nearby metal will change the direction your compass points. A wooden table usually makes a good location, or you can do the experiment outside on the ground.

Notice the behavior of the paper clip. No matter which direction you set it into the water, it will turn to line up north and south. You have built a primitive magnetic compass like that used hundreds of years ago.

Your compass is not just sensitive to the earth's magnetic field. If you bring a magnet near the floating clip, the clip will turn and try to line up with the poles of your magnet. The strength of the magnetic field close to the magnet is much stronger than the earth's field here on the surface of the earth. Of course, the earth's field is much stronger within the earth.

EARTH'S MAGNETIC FIELD

The magnetic field of the earth is created deep within the earth's core. The poles of this magnet are near, but not at exactly the same places as the true north and south axis poles. The true north and south poles of the earth are the poles of the axis that the earth revolves around as it spins. The magnetic north and south poles are presently about 1,200 kilometers (750 miles) away from the axis poles.

The locations of the earth's magnetic poles have slowly

changed over the years and they are still slowly moving today. It has also been discovered that earth's magnetic poles not only move; they have somehow completely reversed polarity many times in earth's history. They appear to switch polarity about every 230,000 years, on the average. The reasons for these polarity changes are not known.

In fact, even the basic cause of the earth's magnetic field is not known for certain. Scientists believe the earth's magnetic field is not caused by a permanent magnet, at least not by ferromagnetism alone. Rather, they think it is caused by some kind of enormous "generator" formed from the moving molten material in the earth's core.

BUILDING AN ELECTROMAGNET

The second method of creating a magnetic force field is with an electric current. This method of creating a magnetic field was first discovered in 1802 by an Italian named Gian Romagnosi. Little attention was given to his discovery until 1820, when it was discovered again by a Danish physicist named Hans Christian Oersted. While giving a lecture on electricity, Oersted discovered that passing an electric current through a wire caused the needle of a nearby compass to turn.

If you have a length of wire, one or two large nails or screws, and a battery such as a "D" size flashlight battery, you can build an electromagnet and repeat Oersted's experiment. The wire must be insulated (it must be coated on the outside with a material such as plastic or varnish). Bare wire will not work. Hardware and radio supply stores usually

94

An electromagnet creates a magnetic field by a flow of electric current. You can make an electromagnet by winding wire around one or two large nails and touching the bare ends of the wire to the terminals of a battery.

stock "hookup" wire in #22 or #20 gauge sizes that will work very well.

You will be winding the wire around the nails. A 16-"penny" (16d) nail makes a handy size, but any large nail, screw, or bolt will do for the center of the electromagnet. This iron "core" will help make a stronger magnet. Hold two nails side by side, with their points in opposite directions.

With one end of the wire sticking out about 20 centimeters (8 inches), start wrapping the wire around and around the core. Wrap it tightly down to one end, then back again in a second layer. Keep wrapping layer after layer. The more turns of wire you have, the stronger the magnetic field it will make.

When all the wire is wrapped, strip or scrape the insulation off the tips of the two wire ends so that they are bare metal. Then hold one wire end to the plus terminal of your battery and the other wire end to the minus terminal. (One caution: don't leave the wire connected to your battery for a long time or the battery will soon run down. Just make a connection when you are actually doing a test.)

A MAGNETIC FIELD FROM ELECTRICITY

To test your electromagnet, touch one end of the magnet to a paper clip, needle, or other small iron or steel object. Does it pick it up? You can also use your new electromagnet to magnetize small pieces of metal. Just rub them against one of the ends as you did with the permanent magnet.

To do Oersted's experiment, bring your electromagnet close to a compass and watch the needle change direction. If you don't have a compass, use the floating paper clip compass.

If you turn the battery around and connect its terminals to the opposite wires, the electric current will flow in the opposite direction. This causes the polarity of the magnetic field to reverse. Try this above the compass. The needle (or the floating clip) will spin around and point in the opposite direction.

Electric motors work on this same principle. The electric

current flowing through coils of wire within the motor is made to reverse direction rapidly and this keeps the moving part of the motor, called the *armature,* spinning.

You have now created a magnetic force from a flow of electricity and seen that this force has the strength to lift small pieces of metal and to cause a compass to turn at some distance. There is something a little eerie about causing an object to move when there appears to be nothing touching and no physical connection of any kind.

Many early scientists had trouble accepting that any force could travel a distance with no material medium to carry it. They thought there must be some medium present that we were unable to detect. They called this mystery medium "ether." Today, we know that no medium is needed, but when you see an electromagnetic field at work, it is easy to understand their feeling of unease at this invisible force that can act at a distance.

ELECTRICITY FROM MAGNETISM

We have made a magnetic field from a flow of electricity. In 1831, an English scientist named Michael Faraday discovered that the opposite can also be done: electricity can be created by a moving magnetic field. A wire conductor that is moved through a magnetic field or a magnetic field that is moved past a wire will cause an electrical current to flow in the wire. This transformation of a magnetic field into an electric current is known as *induction.* (A current is *induced* in the wire.)

The electricity that we use in our homes is created by generators that work by induction. If you built the electromagnet described above, you may have noticed an effect caused by induction. When touching the wire of your electromagnet to the battery in the experiment, did you notice a small spark between the wire and the battery terminal? You may need to be in darkness to see it.

Connect the electromagnet again and notice that the spark happens, not when the wire is touched to the battery, but when it is removed. This spark is caused by induction. (Actually it is *self-induction* in this case because the current is induced back into the same wire that created the magnetic field.)

While current was flowing through the wire, a steady magnetic field surrounded the electromagnet. When you suddenly broke the connection with the battery, the flow of current stopped. This caused the magnetic field to collapse and the moving magnetic field passing through the many coils of wire induced a current in the wire that jumped across the air gap between the wire and the battery terminal.

In the next chapter, we will take a closer look at this electricity you have created and at the ripples that you caused in space with your tiny spark.

9

Electromagnetism: The Electric Force

The electromagnetic force has its source within atoms of matter. Every atom has two different kinds of particles that have electrical charges. There is a compact nucleus at the center that has one or more *protons* that each have a *positive* charge. Circling around the nucleus are one or more *electrons* that each have a *negative* charge. The charge of one proton has the same strength as the charge of one electron.

An electric force field exists between electrical charges that is very much like the magnetic field between the poles of magnets. Opposite charges attract each other with the electric force. The same kind of charges repel each other.

As with magnets, if the same kind of electrical charges are brought together, their fields add to form a stronger overall field. The fields of opposite charges subtract. If the same number of positive and negative charges are present, the overall, net charge will be zero. A normal atom has equal numbers of protons and electrons, so the net charge of a normal atom is zero.

PUSHING AND PULLING WITH THE ELECTRIC FORCE

Early experiments with the electric force were usually done with static electricity. This is still the easiest and safest form to experiment with around the home. Toy balloons are very good for collecting electrical charge. If you have some balloons (round ones are best, but almost any shape will work), inflate two of them and tie a length of thread about 60 centimeters (about 2 feet) long to each one.

The first experiment will be to show how the same kinds of charge repel. First, hold the balloons up by the threads so they hang down together. Since they have no electrical charge yet, the balloons will touch each other. Now let's give them each a charge and see what happens.

Lightly rub each balloon across a wool or nylon carpet or rug, turning it as you do, so that all sides get rubbed. The longer you rub, the greater the electrical charge the balloon will collect. Dry weather, such as a cold winter's day, is the best time. If the weather is damp, you may have to wait for a dryer day to do this experiment.

When both balloons have been thoroughly rubbed all over, hold them up by their strings once more. What happens this time? If the balloons have a good charge, they will not touch. The electric force pushes the balloons apart with greater strength than the force of gravity pulls them down. If you push them together, they will spring apart.

Now let's see how the electric force attracts opposite charges. You may actually be able to feel the electric force. If you have light, dry hair, the balloon will lift some of your hair. Small scraps of paper will also stick to the balloon. Although these objects do not have a net charge themselves,

100

After rubbing on a carpet, two charged balloons push apart because the electric force from the like charges repels. In this photo, one balloon is repelled by the other and also attracted to the girl's dress.

they appear to be opposite to the highly charged balloon.

The most spectacular demonstration of attraction is with water. Adjust the faucet in your kitchen sink or an outside faucet or hose so that there is a very small, but steady, stream of water. A solid stream about the thickness of the lead of a pencil is best.

When you have the water flowing, bring one of the charged balloons near. What happens to the water? If the balloon has a strong charge, you will be able to bend the flow of water toward the balloon. We are so used to seeing water fall straight down, it is a strange sensation to be able to bend a stream of water using a force that we are unable to see.

Turn the balloon around, trying different sides. You will probably find some parts of the balloon that have a greater charge than others. It doesn't hurt if the balloon gets wet. It will still work. If you dry it off, it may lose some charge. If it does, just rub it around on the carpet again to build up the charge.

FRICTIONAL ELECTRICITY

You have just demonstrated the power of the electric force to repel and to attract. You may be wondering why rubbing a balloon across the carpet creates electricity. That is a question that doesn't have a final answer yet. Scientists believe that it is not the rubbing process itself, but rather it is the contact made over a large surface area that actually causes the charge to transfer.

You are not actually creating any new electrical charge by rubbing. Instead, you are moving charge from one material to the other. As the balloon builds up a charge of one

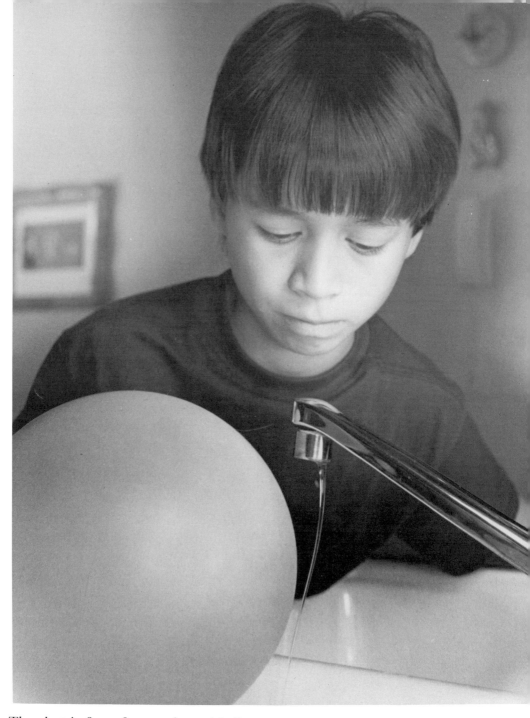

The electric force from a charged balloon attracts a stream of water, causing it to bend.

polarity, the carpet is building up the same amount of charge of the other polarity. Scientists believe that if all of the positive and negative charges in the universe were added, they would balance out to zero.

For any charge to transfer, the two materials must be *insulators*. An insulator is a material that is not able to carry a flow of electric current. Some examples of insulators are glass, rubber, cloth, and paper. To collect a charge by rubbing, the two materials must be different, with different insulating abilities. Rubbing two balloons together, for example, will not build up any charge.

The electrical charge made by rubbing two materials together has the scientific name of *triboelectricity*. The word "tribo" means friction. You may have experienced a charge in yourself after walking across a carpet on a dry winter day or after sliding across a car seat and then touching a door handle.

SEPARATE FORCES

You may want to test for yourself that the magnetic force and the electric force really don't affect each other. The magnetic compass you made by floating a magnetized paper clip makes a good, sensitive detector of magnetic fields. Try bringing one of the charged balloons near the compass and see if the direction of the clip changes. You will discover that it does not. A static electric charge has no effect on a magnetic field.

You might also try bringing a magnet close to the stream of water that you were able to bend so sharply with the electric force. You will find that the stream of water is not bent by the magnetic field. In their static, unmoving forms, the electric force and the magnetic force are completely independent. Let's look now at a case when both electric and magnetic fields are present.

If you have ever made a spark, you have created both types of fields. The spark that jumps from your finger after sliding your feet across the carpet or the tiny spark you made jump between the wire and the battery of the electromagnet sends a wave of force out on a journey across the universe at the speed of light. With your tiny spark, you have just created a weak, but very real, wave that has both an electric and a magnetic field.

ELECTROMAGNETIC RADIATION

A spark is a stream of electrons. This moving charge creates a magnetic field along with its electric one. These two fields travel outward, they *radiate,* in a circular pattern like that of sound waves. The two electric and magnetic fields travel together. They are separate, but inseparable, and together they form a traveling wave known as *electromagnetic radiation.*

Electromagnetic radiation can be created in several different ways and it is familiar to us in many different forms. So many forms, in fact, that we don't always recognize that they are all of the same type. You may be surprised to learn that you have two sensors that are able to detect electromagnetic radiation. We call these sensors eyes, and the radiation they detect is visible light.

Besides visible light, electromagnetic radiation includes radio waves (including television), microwaves, X-rays, ul-

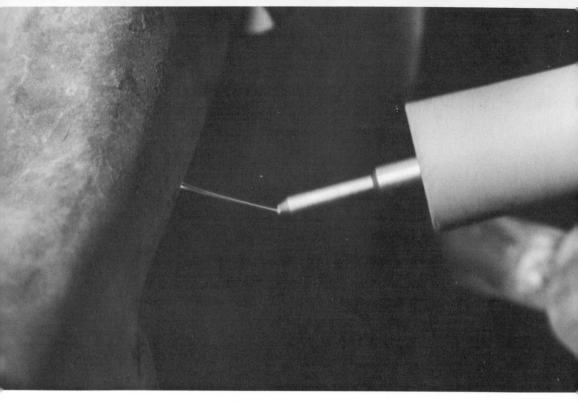

An electric spark starts a wave of electromagnetic radiation on a journey across the universe at the speed of light. This strong spark is from the ignition of an automobile engine.

traviolet rays, and more. We see, communicate, cook our food, check for broken bones, and get sunburned, all by radiation. All of these different "rays" make up what is known as the electromagnetic *spectrum.*

Although there are many different characteristics, all radiation has many of the same features. All radiation can be reflected (bounced back when it strikes a different kind of material). It can be refracted (bent as it enters a material that transmits it at a different speed), and all radiation will show a Doppler effect when there is motion between the source and the receiver. And, all radiation travels at the speed of light.

The interesting thing about radiation is that, unlike sound, it doesn't need any material medium to travel through. In fact, it travels slightly faster through empty space than it does through matter such as air. Light from the sun is bent as it enters the atmosphere near sunrise or sunset. A glass lens works because light travels at a different speed in glass than in air. This speed difference bends the light rays as they enter and leave the lens.

RADIATION PRESSURE

We don't usually think of radiation as having any force. Going outside on a sunny day is not like going out on a windy day. You don't have to lean toward the sun to keep its rays from pushing you over. The force of radiation is so much weaker than all the other forces pushing and pulling on us that we can't feel it.

But radiation does give a weak pressure that can be detected if the other, larger forces are somehow minimized. Light behaves both like waves and like tiny particles. When the tiny particles of light called *photons* strike a surface they exert a tiny force on the surface.

An interesting thing about this force is that it is twice as great against a perfect mirror than against a dull, black surface. A mirror reflects the light. The photons bounce off and an extra "push" is given to the surface in reversing the direction of the photons. A black surface absorbs (catches) the photons and part of their energy is turned into heat.

The mechanical push that we can get from radiation is one form of energy, but it is by far the least important form here on earth. Much more important is the warmth that the sun's radiation brings and the chemical change known as *photosynthesis* that it causes in plants.

By photosynthesis, sunlight enables plants to change water, carbon dioxide, and minerals into oxygen and plant foods. Without this sun-powered "factory," there would be almost no oxygen for us to breathe and no food to eat. Plants are the first step in the food chain that leads to everything you have on your table at dinner. The sun's radiation makes possible every bite of food you eat.

MOLECULE TO MOLECULE

Earlier, we saw that the fundamental force of gravitation created several secondary forces such as the force of buoyancy. The electromagnetic force that binds molecule to molecule also has its secondary forces. If you were able to rest the paper clip on the surface of water when you made the compass, you have seen one of the most interesting of these forces at work. This is the force we will investigate in the next chapter.

10

Surface Forces in Liquids

Have you ever wondered why rain falls in drops? Out of all the possible forms and shapes that water could take on, why does it always fall in little rounded drops? And it isn't only rain that does. Turn a water faucet barely on so that water just drips from the end and you will find that it, too, falls in little drops.

Anytime you try to get water into small amounts by itself, some strange force in the water stubbornly pulls it into little balls. This strange force is not found just in drops. It exists everywhere at a surface where a liquid meets the air. In water, it is actually strong enough to hold up small pieces of metal.

Try this experiment with a paper clip or a pin or needle. Gently lower a paper clip into a bowl or sink of fresh (not soapy) water. Use a fork or a pair of tweezers to set the clip down as flat and as lightly as possible on the surface. If it sinks, try another one or dry that one thoroughly and try again.

When you have a paper clip floating, look closely at the water around it. A magnifying glass will help, but it isn't

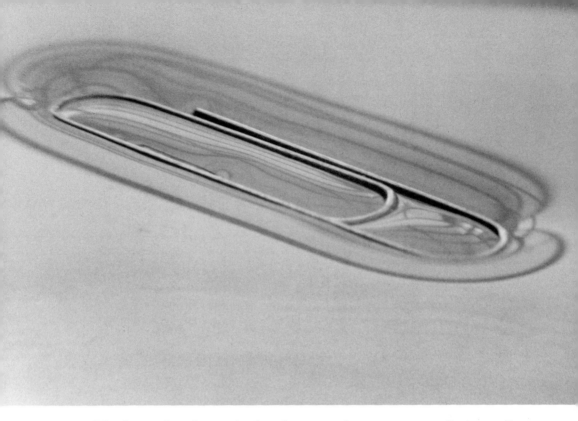

The force of *surface tension* has the strength to support small pieces of metal on top of water. You can "float" a paper clip by gently lowering it into a bowl of water. Notice the bending of the water surface around the clip.

necessary. Notice that the surface of the water is bent where the clip is. The clip isn't floating the way a boat floats. It is held on top of the water by an invisible film. Water spiders and insects sometimes use this same force to stay on top of the water.

This invisible film can be seen another way. Hold another paper clip or the loop of a bent piece of wire in your fingers and slowly lower one end into the water. When the end first begins to enter the water, notice that it makes a "hole" in the water around the end of the clip.

If you lower the clip in a little deeper, the film will suddenly break and the water will rise up around it. This "film" or force is known as *surface tension* and it is caused by electrical forces between the water molecules.

MOLECULAR FORCES

The attractive forces between molecules are electromagnetic forces. These forces are present in all matter, but they are especially strong in water. Although water molecules move freely about and around each other, each molecule is strongly attracted to other molecules on every side.

Within the liquid, the attractive forces pulling on each molecule are balanced in all directions. Around each molecule, there are other molecules pulling from above, below, and on all sides.

At the surface of the liquid, however, the forces pulling on each molecule are not balanced. There are only molecules of the liquid below and on the sides of each surface molecule. The attraction by the molecules of air above the liquid are much weaker than those within the liquid. These forces pulling from only one side act like a kind of invisible "net" stretched across the surface. Tightening or pulling by a force is called *tension*.

SURFACE TENSION AT WORK

Surface tension pulls the liquid into a shape that has the smallest surface area. The geometrical shape with the smallest surface area for its volume is a sphere. A ball is one example of a sphere. This is why droplets of water form into little balls. When they fall as rain through the air, the force of the airflow around them shapes raindrops into their familiar rounded-on-the-bottom, pointed-on-the-top, shape.

For larger amounts of water, the weight of the water is greater than the surface tension can hold. If poured into a container, the pull of gravity will force the water down into the shape of the container. If there were no gravity, or if you were an astronaut in orbit, water would float around the room in little balls, like water-filled balloons, only without the balloon.

There is another easy experiment you can do with surface tension, using a penny or other small coin. See how high you can "stack" water on the penny before the weight of the water breaks the surface tension film. Lay the penny on its side and drop water onto the penny from an eye dropper, a drinking straw, or from a small cup.

You will be able to build a drop of water several times the thickness of the penny before it bursts. You can also do this experiment by resting the penny on the end of your finger and holding it under a dripping faucet.

We see the effects of surface tension dozens of times a day. When we pour milk from a milk bottle or carton, the milk pours out in a column of liquid. Drinking fountains shoot an arch of liquid water up for us to drink. Without surface tension, milk and water would probably pour out as a fine spray or mist instead of a column of liquid.

While surface tension helps us in most ways, it works against us in cleaning. By itself, water is not a very good cleaner. Surface tension keeps water bunched up into drops and doesn't allow it to penetrate into the fibers of clothes

112

Surface tension pulls water into the shape of a sphere. You can "stack" water onto a penny with an eye dropper or a drinking straw.

very well. If we washed dirty or greasy clothes or dishes in plain water, much of the dirt and grease would still be there when we finished. To make water into a good cleaner, something is needed to break down the surface tension. We need a soap or detergent.

LOWERING SURFACE TENSION:
DETERGENTS AT WORK

Try one more experiment with the floating paper clip. Add a drop of liquid detergent to the water on the opposite side of the bowl. Liquid detergent such as dish washing detergent is best, but rubbing a bar of hand soap in the water will also work. Watch closely when you add the detergent because the change it makes will happen very quickly.

Almost as soon as the detergent touches the water, a ripple seems to rush across the surface of the water and the paper clip sinks to the bottom. Try to float the clip again and you will find that it can't be done. It will go straight to the bottom every time.

Soaps and detergents lower the surface tension of water by breaking up the "net" of forces connecting the water molecules. Soap and detergent molecules are in the form of long chains with different kinds of molecules on each end of the chain.

On one end, there are molecules that are attracted to water. These are called *hydrophillic* ("hydro" means water and "phillic" means loving). On the opposite end, there are molecules that repel (that push away) water. These are called *hydrophobic* ("phobic" means fearing).

When soap is put into water, the hydrophillic end of the soap molecules penetrate into the water droplets and the hydrophobic ends stay on the outside. The soap molecules wedge themselves between the water molecules and break up the forces linking the water molecules together. This lowers the strength of the surface tension.

THE FORCE OF ADHESION

Water molecules not only have a great force of attraction for each other; they also have an attraction for certain other materials. The molecules of glass, for example, are strongly attracted by water.

Partly fill a clean water glass with water and look closely at the surface near the edge where the water meets the glass. The surface will be curved upward slightly. The water is somehow pulling itself up in spite of the force of gravity pulling it down.

This attraction to a different kind of molecule is called *adhesion*. When a liquid sticks (adheres) to a solid, such as the water to glass, it is said to "wet" the surface of the solid. Liquids only wet certain kinds of materials. Most plastics, for example, will usually not show the same effect.

You probably make some use of adhesion almost every day. Have you ever mopped up a spill with a paper towel? A paper towel or tissue soaks up water by adhesion. Put one corner of a paper towel into a cup of water and the water will quickly start to climb up out of the cup, wetting the towel. Paper towels and tissues are designed to have a high adhesion for water molecules.

THE CAPILLARY EFFECT

Adhesion is much more important to us than just paper towels. Have you ever wondered how trees are able to carry water and nutrients from their roots up to their top leaves and branches? Plants have no heart to pump liquids through their systems as animals do. Most plants depend on the ability of water to make this uphill journey against the pull of gravity.

Look at the curved level of the water in the glass again. Imagine what would happen if the glass were made narrower and narrower until it became a thin tube. When the opposite sides of the glass became close enough together that the curve of water next to one side touched the curve of water next to the opposite side, we would see the level of the water start to rise up into the tube.

The narrower we made this tube, the higher we would see the level of the water climb. Adhesion pulls the water up the sides and surface tension keeps the water from separating, so the center is also pulled up. The water acts almost as if it were forced upward from a pump.

This action is called the *capillary effect* or *capillarity*, and a narrow tube that carries liquids is called a capillary tube. Inside plants such as trees, there is material called *vascular tissue* that has millions of tiny tubes. These tubes carry water and dissolved minerals up from the roots to the leaves and also carry food back from the leaves to the rest of the plant. Without capillarity, there would be few plants as we know them.

ADHESION IN SOLIDS

Adhesion between molecules is at work wherever you see any two materials touching. In liquids, it causes the useful capillary action as well as making our paper towels and tissues absorbent.

Adhesion is also at work wherever two solid materials touch. As you hold this book, some of the molecules of the skin of your hands are bonded to the molecules of the book. We will take a closer look at this bonding when we investigate the force of friction next.

Adhesion and surface tension combine to cause the *capillary action* that pulls water from the roots of plants up to their highest leaves. This close-up photo of a slice of celery shows the tiny tubes that carry water.

116

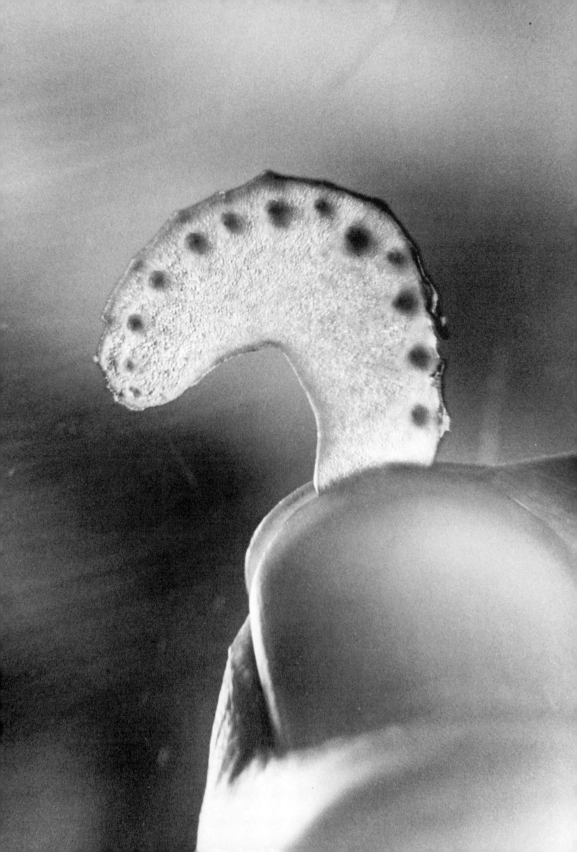

11

Against All Motion: Friction

Press the palms of your hands together and rub them rapidly back and forth. Feel the heat? This heating is caused by the force of *friction* between your two hands. At the molecular level, strange and violent things are happening to the skin of your hands because of friction.

As you rub one hand across the other, bits of skin of one hand become bonded, actually sticking to the skin of the other. As your hands move past each other, these bits of skin are then ripped apart again. The work done in tearing apart these bonds produces heat and this is the heat that you feel. Don't worry. The amount of skin that becomes stuck together and torn apart is extremely small.

Friction is a secondary force that is present when two different objects or materials touch each other. It is caused by the same force of adhesion that makes water curve upward at the sides of a glass. The fundamental force that causes adhesion is the electromagnetic force that binds molecules together.

Friction is a different kind of force than the others that we have seen because it never causes any motion. It always

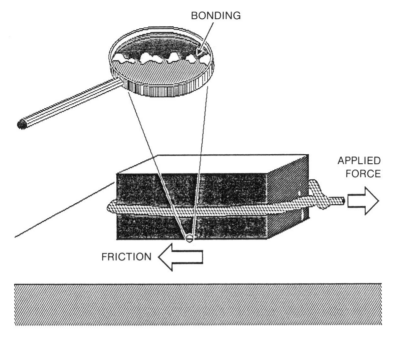

BONDING

APPLIED
FORCE

FRICTION

The force of *friction* between two surfaces is caused by microscopic high points between two materials bonding together. Friction always acts in the opposite direction of any applied force.

acts against any attempt to move the surface of one object over another. In the science of mechanics, friction is treated like any other force that may be pulling or pushing on an object, but with one big difference. Friction always has a direction opposite to that of any movement.

A MIXED BLESSING

It is safe to say that we couldn't live without friction. Have you ever tried to walk on ice? Without friction, every surface would be perfectly slippery, far more slippery than the

119

smoothest sheet of ice. We wouldn't be able to stand without falling. Our hands would be nearly useless for grasping things. The only way we could hold something would be to cup our hands around it. Squeezing an object would only make it shoot out of our fingers.

We take friction so much for granted, it is difficult to imagine a world without it. The design of almost every kind of transportation from automobiles to skateboards would have to be completely changed. Even the way we build houses would have to be changed.

Without friction, most of today's houses would fall apart. It is friction that holds the nails in boards. Without it, all of the nails would just slide back out again and the boards would separate.

We need friction for just about everything, but there are a few cases where we would like to make it much less. To motors and machinery of all kinds, friction is an enemy. Any place where moving surfaces touch, friction causes wear. Without friction, cars, airplanes, and toys would last many times longer than they do today.

Because friction opposes other forces, extra power is needed to overcome it. An estimated 20 percent of all the fuel used by cars and trucks goes to overcome the force of friction. Without friction, every machine would be more efficient and enormous amounts of fuel would be saved every year.

This would not only help conservation, but would also reduce the pollution caused by burning oil and coal. Friction is definitely a mixed blessing. We need it to live, but there are times and places where we would like to be able to reduce it.

THE TWO FRICTIONS

Friction is usually divided into two types: *static friction* and sliding or *kinetic friction*. Static friction is the force between two surfaces that are not moving relative to each other. As an example, think of a book resting on top of a table. The force between the book and the table is static friction.

Kinetic friction is the force between surfaces where there is movement between them. If you pushed on the book hard enough to start it sliding, the force between the moving book and the table is kinetic friction.

Since friction acts only to oppose motion, we can't measure its force directly. To measure the frictional force, we must start some motion using another force and then measure that applied force.

The strength of static friction is the amount of applied force that is needed to just start an object moving. The strength of kinetic friction is the amount of applied force that is needed to keep the object moving at a constant speed.

Static and kinetic friction are the same basic force with the same causes, but they are given different names because they almost always have different values. Static friction is almost always greater than kinetic friction. A greater force is needed to start an object moving than to keep it moving.

LEONARDO AND THE LAWS OF FRICTION

About 500 years ago, well before Galileo's and Newton's studies of forces, two laws of friction were discovered experimentally by Leonardo da Vinci in Italy. Even today, the study of friction is still largely based on experiments.

There is no single mathematical law or theory that accurately describes the frictional force.

The two laws that Leonardo da Vinci discovered about friction remain true today. He found that:

1. The amount of surface area that is touching between two objects has little effect on friction.

2. The force of friction depends directly on the force (usually the weight) that presses the two objects together. Doubling the weight, for example, doubles the amount of friction.

Try an experiment to test Leonardo's laws of friction for yourself. If you happen to have a small spring scales (such as a postal scales) in your home, you can use it to measure exact values for the frictional forces. If you don't have such a scales, don't worry. It's easy and more fun to make your own scales for comparing force strength.

All you need to make a scales are a couple of pieces of string, a rubber band, and a sheet of lined notebook paper. Force strength will be compared by measuring how far the force stretches the rubber band. A greater force will stretch the band a greater distance than a lesser force.

This simple scales won't give you a measurement of force in pounds or newtons and it isn't very linear (that is, the stretch distance of the band won't necessarily double if the force is doubled), but it is sensitive and reliable for telling which of several forces is greater.

Cut one piece of string about 60 centimeters (about 2 feet) long. Tie a large loop in one end and tie the other end to the rubber band. Cut another piece of string about 8 centimeters (3 inches) long and tie one end of it to the opposite side of the rubber band.

A simple scales for experimenting with friction can be made with a rubber band, string, and a piece of notebook paper. A greater force stretches the rubber band a greater distance, indicated by numbers on the paper.

With a ruler or straight edge, draw a line down the center of the notebook paper from top to bottom. Tape the short piece of string to the line at a position near the top of the paper.

Put the tape over the string just behind the rubber band so the end of the string hangs over the top edge of the paper. This will be the handle you will use to pull with.

Lay the longer piece of string and the rubber band down the line that you drew and pull it just enough to straighten the rubber band. With a pencil, make a mark across the line at one of the paper's ruled lines nearest the knot where the long string is tied to the rubber band.

Label this first mark with a "0". Then make marks at every ruled line down the page, labeling them "1, 2, 3 . . ." and so on. As the rubber band stretches to greater length, the knot will be near higher numbers. Your force scales is now finished and ready to be used.

TESTING LEONARDO'S LAWS

To test the first law of friction, you will need some object with sides of different areas. A book that is two or three centimeters (an inch or so) thick will work very well. Choose a book that doesn't have a jacket, so the sides and edges of the cover are made of the same material.

Lay the book on the top of a table and loop the string around it. Now pull with a steady force on the string. Keep the string lined up with the labeled scale, and watch the place where the knot is located.

The first thing you will see is the difference between static and kinetic friction. The force will be greatest (the knot will be pulled to the highest number) an instant before the book starts to slide.

Once the book starts sliding, try to keep it moving at a steady speed and see where the knot is located. You will find it is next to a lower number for this kinetic friction case than it was for the static case.

The first law of friction says that the area of contact doesn't change the frictional force. To test this, stand the book on end and again loop the string around it. Now pull again until the book is sliding. Is the knot next to the same number that it was when the book was lying on its side?

124

You will probably find that it is close, but perhaps not at exactly the same place as before. An important thing to remember is that the "laws" of friction are not exact. There are many exceptions, especially for soft materials.

The first law of friction is a very strange one. Friction is caused by the adhesion between molecules of the two different materials. If there are more molecules of material touching, you would expect more friction. Instead, you found that the friction was about the same. We will see why scientists think this happens after we test the second law.

The second law says that friction depends directly upon the force pressing the two surfaces together. Since our scales is only good for making "greater than" or "less than" kinds of comparisons, we can't test this accurately, but we can see if friction increases with greater weight.

Place the book back on its side again, and again see where the knot is located when the book is sliding. Now place another book on top of the first one. What happens to the force? You will find that it is much greater, just as the law predicted.

You may want to test your book and scales on other surfaces to see if they change the frictional force. If you can, try both a rougher surface and a smoother surface than the original table top. Our "common sense" tells us that an object should slide more easily (the friction will be lower) on a smooth surface.

You may be surprised to find that a smoother surface does not always make the friction lower. A glass table top, for example, will usually show a greater frictional force than a wooden one. Friction doesn't always behave as we might expect.

MICROSCOPIC "MOUNTAINS"

The first law of friction seems to say that the area of contact (the parts that are touching) isn't important to friction. It is believed that the contact area really is very important, but that the real area that is touching between two objects is much less than it seems. A surface that seems flat and smooth to our eyes is actually covered with microscopic "mountains" and "valleys."

When two surfaces are pressed together, as your book on a table, it is only these high points of each that touch. Because their area is very small, the pressure on these points is enormous. Even materials as hard as brick or steel or concrete bend slightly and as they bend, more points of each touch.

Scientists believe that the actual area touching depends directly upon the force pressing them together. Stacking a second book on top of the first doubles the friction because it causes about twice as many of the microscopic peaks to touch and this doubles the real area in contact. Turning the book from its side to its end didn't change the friction very much because the real contact area stayed about the same.

When one surface slides over the other, the molecules on these points of one material are pressed so tightly against the molecules of the other that the two materials become welded together at these points. As the surfaces slide on, these points are then sheared apart. Some of the kinetic energy, the energy of motion of the moving object, is changed into heat by the work done in forming and shearing these bonds.

126

REDUCING FRICTION

Finding ways to reduce friction has concerned engineers from the earliest civilizations and the work continues today. While many advances in materials and designs have been made over the centuries, there are still two basic ways of making friction less.

The first method is that of *lubrication.* Lubrication was used by the ancient Egyptians over 4,000 years ago to help them move large blocks of stone to build pyramids and statues. To make it possible for teams of slaves to slide heavy blocks into place, they poured some type of oil in front of the stones. You know from experience that oil or water on a surface makes it slippery. A "slippery" surface is one with very little friction.

Most lubricants are liquid, although gas is sometimes used when there are very high speeds involved. You will remember that the molecules of liquids slide easily over each other. When a liquid lubricant is put between two solid surfaces, the surfaces are "floated" apart so that there are fewer or perhaps no areas of the two solids touching each other. No more adhesion takes place between the solids. The lubricant's molecules do all the work of sliding.

The other method of reducing friction is to roll rather than slide. *Rolling friction* is usually lower than sliding friction. Using rolling to reduce friction is as old or perhaps older than the use of lubrication. Even before the wheel and axle were invented, log rollers were used beneath heavy objects to move them with less effort. Today, our civilization depends heavily on wheels for transportation of all kinds. Even

Rolling friction is almost always less than sliding friction. Put a book on any kind of rollers and the rubber band scales barely stretches when the book is pulled.

aircraft need wheels for takeoffs and landings.

At the molecular level, the adhesion that takes place between two materials is the same, no matter whether there is rolling or sliding taking place. Rolling friction is less than sliding friction because of the way the bonds are broken.

The molecular bonds that have adhered between the two surfaces are pulled or peeled apart when a wheel or roller turns, rather than sheared apart as they are when there is sliding. This pulling or peeling takes less force than shearing, so the friction is less.

FORCES AT WORK

It is sometimes difficult to imagine forces at work because much of the real action happens outside the range of our senses. The forces themselves are usually invisible and, also, forces like friction are working at the microscopic and molecular levels.

"Seeing" forces at work takes some imagination and the ability to spot small clues in the way materials look and act. In the final chapter, we will look more closely at the part imagination plays in seeing into the hidden world of forces.

12

The Hidden World of Forces

Everywhere you look, everything that you see and touch has some kind of force at work on and within it. You have now read about and experimented with some of the more familiar forces. There are still many others. There are many more than a book this length could possibly cover and there is much more that could be said about each one. Hopefully, your curiosity about forces will lead you to more reading and more experiments.

Knowing something about forces can give you a kind of "X-ray vision" (actually, more like an X-ray imagination). This vision, sharpened by your knowledge, lets you see through the surface appearance of things to find the underlying structure and causes beneath.

This is the way a scientist or an engineer looks at the world, but this kind of vision is not limited to science. An artist painting a picture of a person imagines the bone and muscle structure beneath the skin. If the artist doesn't have this knowledge of anatomy, the painting is likely to look flat and lifeless.

An architect looks at a building in the same sort of way, imagining the supporting steel girders and beams beneath the glass and brick covering. You can probably think of many more examples. In every job and in every hobby, there is specialized knowledge that adds another dimension to a person's vision.

Knowing something about what causes forces and how they work can add depth to your everyday experiences. Everywhere you look, there are clues that tell you forces are at work. Their signs are often simple and strikingly beautiful if you know what to look for. Some of the clues to look for have been mentioned in the earlier chapters of this book. With practice, you will be able to find many more.

FORCE, AREA, AND PRESSURE

Remember that area is the connection between force and pressure. Look for things that use area to change one into the other. Pressure-to-force transformers are the most common. Examples of areas that change pressure to force are the sails of boats and the wings of airplanes.

In machinery and tools, look for force and pressure multipliers. You will see large-to-small and small-to-large areas used to multiply pressure or force somewhere in almost every mechanical device. In hand tools, look for large surface areas for the hand to grasp and small areas for the working point or end. Some examples are knives, scissors, and thumbtacks.

In machines and devices that use liquids or gases under pressure, look for cylinders that have pistons inside that multiply force. You will often see small cylinders that pump liquid or gas into a larger cylinder or container. Some examples are tire pumps and lifts for cars.

GRAVITATION AND MECHANICS

Look for situations that involve both weight and acceleration. Remember the dual nature of mass that attracts other objects with the force of gravity and that resists an acceleration. This makes heavy objects fall at the same rate as light ones (without air resistance).

Two familiar examples are the pendulums of grandfather clocks and the swings on a children's playground. The time for a pendulum to make a back and forth swing will be the same whether a pendulum is heavy or light or whether the child on the swing is large or small.

GRAVITY-CAUSED PRESSURES

Gravity causes an increase in pressure with depth in all materials. Look for some of the effects of this pressure. The force of buoyancy from this pressure pushes less dense objects upward. Boats floating and balloons rising are among the most common examples of buoyancy at work.

Notice the pressure change on your ears when you drive up a hill or go to the top of a tall building or dive to the bottom of a swimming pool. Look also for ways in which we use this pressure gradient. Depth gauges, altimeters, and barometers are some examples.

Also, look for examples of pressure put to work pumping

There are clues everywhere that forces are at work. With gravitation, look for situations where both gravity and acceleration are at work. For playground swings of the same length, the time of a back and forth swing is the same whether the child is heavy or light.

liquids with siphon action. Two common examples around the house are toilets and the curved "traps" in drain pipes.

MOTION-CAUSED FORCES IN LIQUIDS AND GASES

Any time a solid object moves through a liquid or gas or there is a flow over an object, the force of lift will be present. The shape of an object is usually a good clue to the way it develops and uses this force.

Some examples are the curved shapes of airplane wings, propellers, and racing car bodies and fins. (A racing car has a downward "lift" to hold the car on the track.)

Notice the shapes of solids that have a flow of liquid or gas over them. They will often be curved. The curve of this jet aircraft wing creates lift from the flow of air around it.

TRAVELING PRESSURE WAVES

When you hear a sound, notice its source. Something must disturb the air to make sound. Usually the sound source will be something with a back-and-forth vibration. There is often a connection between size and pitch. A large object will often vibrate more slowly and this makes a lower-pitched sound.

Look for situations where you can see that the speed of sound is much slower than the speed of light. Thunder and lightning are probably the most spectacular example. Building construction sites are often another good place. If you can see a worker hammering some distance away, notice the difference between when you see the hammer hit and when you hear the sound.

Listen for reflections. The sides of large buildings are often good for echoes. Listen also for the way reflections in different places change the way voices or noises sound. Could you tell what kind of place you were in if you couldn't see?

Try to detect the Doppler effect anytime there is high speed motion. You can often hear a drop in the pitch of the noises from a car as it goes by on a highway or street or from a jet plane as it passes overhead at low altitude.

ELECTRICITY AND MAGNETISM

Never pass up a chance to play with a magnet. There is always something new to try and something new to learn. For example, you might experiment with how different materials pass or block a magnetic field.

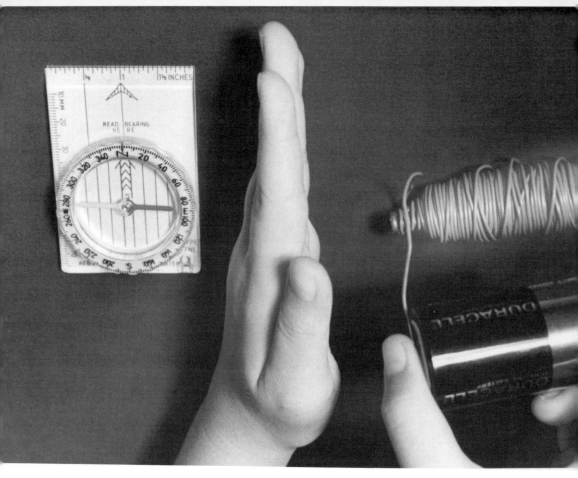

There are many experiments you can do with magnets. For example, you will find that most materials pass a magnetic field. The field from this magnet is able to pass through the person's hand and turn the needle of the compass away from north.

Look for ways that we use magnetic force. Some examples are the decorative magnets used to stick notes onto the refrigerator, some kinds of cabinet latches, metal detectors that are used to search for treasure, and all kinds of electric motors. In any device that uses magnetic force, try to see if the force is created by ferromagnetism or electromagnetism. Look for ways that the electric force can be created. Static electricity made by rubbing two insulators together is the most common way. See if you can identify the insulators. Does the force repel or attract other objects?

Look for different ways that electromagnetic radiation is used. Our vision, microwave ovens, radio and television, X-rays used in medicine and baggage inspection in airports are only a few examples. Try to discover how the radiation is generated. Is it man-made or natural?

Notice how light is refracted as it passes through curved glass lenses, bottles, and drinking glasses. Remember that refraction is caused by the different speed of the radiation in the different materials. Notice also what reflections from mirrors do to the image that you see.

SURFACE FORCES IN LIQUIDS

Any place that a liquid meets a gas or a solid, look for surface forces at work. Surface tension acts like an invisible net around the liquid. We see it most commonly in water. Notice how water pulls itself into drops or into a stream from a drinking fountain.

Look for adhesion at the edges of containers where the liquid meets the side. If there is adhesion between the liquid and the solid, the liquid will curve upward. If there is not, it will curve downward. Plants live by this capillary action. When you see a tall tree, imagine water being pulled all the way from the roots to the top branches.

FRICTION

Friction works both for and against us. Look for clues in the design of machines that tell you whether the designer

Look for the effects of adhesion and surface tension on liquids, especially any place that a liquid and a solid meet. In this photo, water seems to pull itself up from the surface to stick to the spoon.

was trying to make friction greater or less. Soft, flexible materials that mold to the other object's shape are often used to make friction greater. Some examples are the rubber tires of cars and bicycles and rubber handles on tools and bicycle handle bars.

Friction is reduced by lubrication and rolling instead of sliding. Look for places where lubricating materials such as oil or grease are used. You have probably used lubrication yourself many times. Have you ever rubbed a playground slide with wax paper to make it more slippery? Or sprayed water on a sheet of plastic to make a slide on the grass?

SCIENCE AROUND US

If you did many of the experiments in this book, you know that quite a lot of science can be done with "instruments" as simple and as cheap as paper clips, balloons, and rubber bands. Everyone everywhere can experiment with science to some degree.

Too often, movies and television picture science as something that can only be practiced in a well-equipped laboratory by white-coated "scientists." Nothing could be further from the truth. Real science can't be separated from real life.

As you did the experiments in this book, you probably didn't find any that were completely strange or unexpected. Both the materials and the results were familiar because, in a way, you have been experimenting with science and especially with forces all of your life.

You may have discovered, however, that there are some interesting forces at work in the most common places. Too often, we stop noticing the things around us just because they are so familiar. We all need to stop from time to time and look at our world in a new, fresh way. One of the wonderful things about science is its ability to give us new ways of thinking about old, familiar things.

The most important scientific "tool" of all is not anything

that you can buy. It is your own mind. Your thoughts and ideas are the keys that can unlock mysteries. Hopefully, this book has answered some of the questions that you may have had about forces.

More important than answers, though, it is hoped that this book has stimulated new questions, perhaps even a few that you may not have thought to ask before. There are still many mysteries about forces. The answers will come only if we ask the right questions. In the search for understanding, questions are perhaps the most powerful "force" of all.

INDEX

Page numbers in italics indicate illustrations

142